A·SHORT HISTORY OF THE WORLD

Internet Links

We hope this short introduction will inspire you to explore the immense history of the world further. At the Usborne Quicklinks website, you'll find recommendations of carefully selected websites to help you on your way. Turn to the back of this book to find out more...

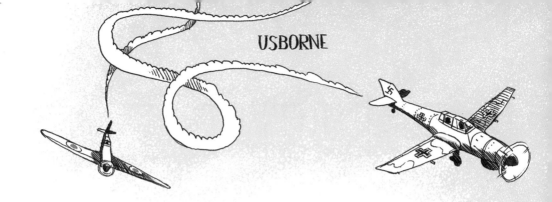

A SHORT HISTORY
OF THE
WORLD

Ruth Brocklehurst & Henry Brook

Illustrated by Adam Larkum

Designed by
Alice Reese & Hayley Wells

Edited by Jane Chisholm & Dr. Anne Millard

CONTENTS

PART ONE

THE ANCIENT WORLD

From the Ice Age

Hungry Ice-Age
hunters

DATES IN THIS BOOK

Dates shown with the letters 'BC' are from the time *Before Christ* was born. They are counted back from the year 1BC. Today, many people, especially non-Christians, use 'BCE' instead of 'BC'. This stands for *Before* the *Common Era*. The letter 'c.' before a date means the precise date is not known.

PREHISTORIC PEOPLE

People have been around for an unimaginably long time. There were human-like creatures in Africa over five million years ago. But modern humans, or *Homo sapiens sapiens* to use our scientific name, first appeared around 150,000 years ago.

HISTORY IS...

...the study of the past through written records, as well as things or traces people left behind. But hunter-gatherers didn't know how to read and write, so historians refer to this period as 'prehistory'.

Spreading out

Our prehistoric ancestors lived in small groups, moving from place to place, gathering plants to eat, fishing and hunting. They slept in caves or shelters made from branches and animal skins.

Life was tough. The search for food took these hunter-gatherers from Africa into Asia and then to Europe, and some even reached as far as Australia.

Around 30,000 years ago, the world was in the grip of a period of extreme cold called an ice age. Vast areas of land were frozen over and sea levels were so low that people were even able to cross from Asia to America on foot.

7

Woolly mammoth (now extinct)

Ice-Age hunters

There isn't much time for the finer things in life when you're always looking for your next meal. But Ice-Age hunters weren't just survivors – they were inventors, artists and craftworkers, too.

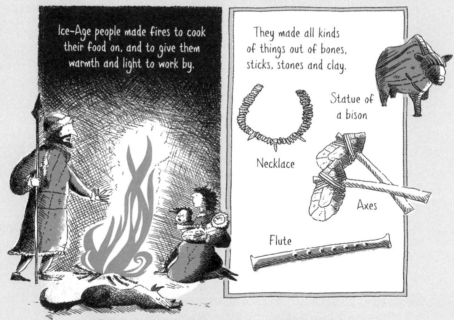

Ice-Age people made fires to cook their food on, and to give them warmth and light to work by.

They made all kinds of things out of bones, sticks, stones and clay.

Statue of a bison

Necklace

Axes

Flute

They tamed dogs to help them hunt – and for company.

As the Ice Age began to thaw, temperatures gradually rose, and lush grassland and forests replaced ice and snow. New animals arrived, and the hunter-gatherers followed after them. Sometimes, food was in such plentiful supply that people began to settle in more permanent camps. The Ice Age was finally over.

FARMING AND SETTLING

Ancient wheat
called einkorn

The hunter-gatherer way of life continued for thousands of years, but in some areas, people began to settle into a new way of life – farming. It started first in the Middle East, where people kept animals and cultivated early forms of wheat, barley and vegetables. The first crop in Africa was sorghum grain, and in China it was rice.

Towns and trading

Farmers soon found they could produce more food if they worked together. So communities expanded into villages and towns, and kings and priests emerged to take charge.

In places where they were able to grow more food than they needed, people now had time to develop crafts such as pottery, spinning, weaving and, later, metalwork. Some even became rich trading their goods and produce.

9

EARLY CIVILIZATIONS

The next big change in the way people lived came as they became more organized, built great cities and vast monuments, and when they invented writing. Historians call this civilization.

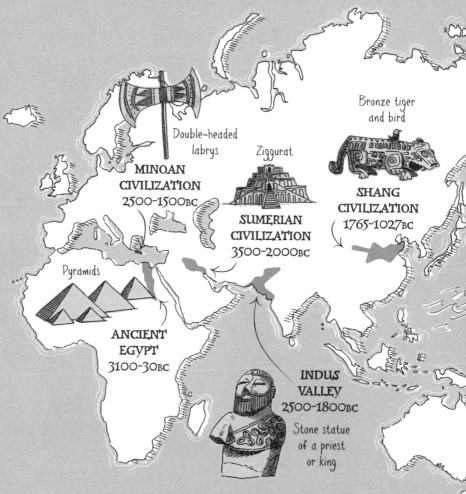

Double-headed labrys

MINOAN CIVILIZATION
2500-1500BC

Ziggurat

Bronze tiger and bird

SHANG CIVILIZATION
1765-1027BC

SUMERIAN CIVILIZATION
3500-2000BC

Pyramids

ANCIENT EGYPT
3100-30BC

INDUS VALLEY
2500-1800BC

Stone statue of a priest or king

10

Many of the world's first civilizations began in fertile valleys of great rivers. The very first of these, the Sumerian civilization, grew up in the Middle East, more than 5,500 years ago in 3500BC.

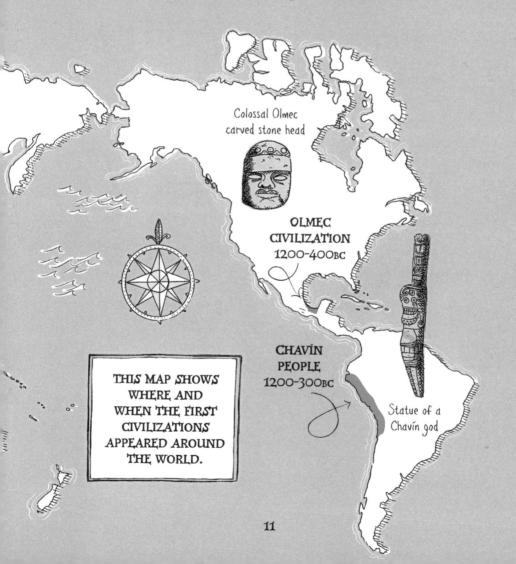

Colossal Olmec carved stone head

OLMEC CIVILIZATION 1200-400BC

CHAVÍN PEOPLE 1200-300BC

Statue of a Chavín god

THIS MAP SHOWS WHERE AND WHEN THE FIRST CIVILIZATIONS APPEARED AROUND THE WORLD.

Sumerian civilization

Mud. The people of Sumer, on the banks of the Tigris and Euphrates rivers, had a lot of mud. But they were inventive with it.

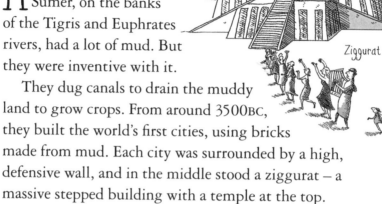

Ziggurat

They dug canals to drain the muddy land to grow crops. From around 3500BC, they built the world's first cities, using bricks made from mud. Each city was surrounded by a high, defensive wall, and in the middle stood a ziggurat – a massive stepped building with a temple at the top.

Kings and queens wore elaborate gold crowns.

Sumerians took goods to the temple - these were collected as tax.

SUMERIAN INVENTORS...

...weren't only inventive with mud. They invented lots of other things too:

* Wheels for carts
* Wheels for making pottery
* The 60-minute hour

* The 12-month calendar
* The 360-degree circle
* Their own system of writing

Ruling Mesopotamia

Sumer was in the southern part of a region known as Mesopotamia – meaning 'the land between two rivers'. Each Sumerian city was a separate state with its own ruler. Sometimes, one city would capture another, but no one ever ruled the whole region – that is, until Sargon stormed in. Sargon was a powerful army commander from Akkad, to the north of Sumer. He conquered city after city, and by 2350BC most of Mesopotamia was under his rule.

Hammurabi

Around 2000BC, Mesopotamia was invaded by desert tribes known as the Amorites, who set up several small city states. Eventually, Hammurabi, ruler of one of the cities, Babylon, conquered the other Amorite kings and seized power over the region. To keep order, he enforced strict laws and punishments. These laws were carved on stone pillars displayed in public places, so everyone knew he was in charge.

SOME OF HAMMURABI'S LAWS

If a surgeon killed a patient during an operation, he'd have his hand cut off.

If a house collapsed killing a person, the architect would be put to death.

Kidnapping, thieving, lying in court and offending the gods were all punishable by death.

Life on the Nile

Every summer in Egypt, the river Nile flooded its banks, leaving behind a rich mud that made the soil fertile for farming. This helped Africa's first civilization to grow. Ancient Egypt lasted as a kingdom over 3,000 years, and many of its monuments are still standing today.

Ancient Egypt was ruled by rich, powerful kings we call pharaohs.

The Egyptians worshipped many gods and goddesses. They even believed the pharaoh was descended from a god.

Huge temples were built for each god. Only priests were allowed inside, but on festival days they held parades outside.

Statue of a god in a shrine

The Egyptians believed in life after death. Bodies of important people were preserved and buried in brightly painted coffins, in tombs filled with things they might need to enjoy the next life.

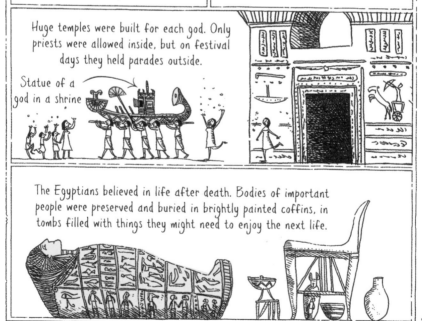

Some pharaohs' tombs were housed inside towering pyramids that seemed to reach for the sun. These took great engineering skill to design, and up to 20 years to build.

Pyramids

Pharaohs after 1500BC didn't have pyramids. Their tombs were carved deep into the desert rock in a place called the Valley of the Kings.

Over many centuries, most pharaohs' tombs were robbed, but in the 1920s King Tutankhamun's was found untouched.

Among its treasures was a stunning gold funeral mask.

Warrior pharaohs led their soldiers into battles, on land and at sea, conquering many surrounding territories.

But they came under attack too. From the 700sBC, Egypt was invaded and conquered several times. In 30BC, 3,000 years of Egyptian independence finally ended, when the Romans (see pages 43–45) took control.

The last pharaoh, Queen Cleopatra, killed herself – possibly with snake venom – rather than submit to Roman rule.

Cities of the Indus Valley

Keeping clean was central to people's lives in the Indus Valley. They built cities with wide, straight streets and public wells. Almost every house had a bathroom and toilet connected to sewers under the roads.

Craftworkers in markets and workshops wove cotton cloth, worked metal and made pots and beads, while merchants sailed as far as Sumer to trade their goods.

In Mohenjo-daro, one of the largest cities, there was a fortress perched on a man-made hill. Inside were grain stores, meeting rooms and a large bathhouse that was probably used by priest-kings for religious ceremonies.

Priests bathed in a sacred pool

Around 1800BC, people began to abandon the Indus cities. No one knows why, but it's possible they over-farmed the land and cut down too many trees, leaving the valley barren and vulnerable to flooding.

Standing stones

In northern Europe, people didn't have writing or cities, but they had a distinct culture. Farmers began building massive stone monuments for religious meetings. Some, such as the rows of standing stones at Carnac in France, and the stone circles of Stonehenge in England and the Ring of Brodgar on the Scottish island of Orkney, still loom over the landscape today.

Some of these stones weigh as much as 370 men!

These people buried their dead in barrows – stone tombs covered with earth mounds. At first, lots of people were buried together in long barrows. Later, barrows were round, and held just a single very important person. All this took a lot of organization, time and effort, so you could say these monument builders had their own form of civilization.

The invention of writing

Most early civilizations developed their own forms of writing, but over the centuries, many of these were forgotten. Historians and code experts have spent years trying to decipher the writing left behind on stone or clay tablets, scrolls, buildings and other objects – the earliest records of people's lives, from important events and law codes, to shopping lists and who owned what.

The **SUMERIANS** invented writing around 3300BC. Officials drew simple pictures onto soft clay tablets that were then baked hard in the sun, to keep records of who had paid their taxes.

Picture writing

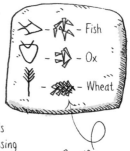

- Fish
- Ox
- Wheat

By 3100BC, pictures had been replaced with symbols known as cuneiform writing. These were made by pressing the end of a wedge-shaped tool into the clay.

Cuneiform writing

Writing was invented in **ANCIENT EGYPT** at around the same time. Scribes wrote using picture symbols, known as hieroglyphs, to record everything from business deals to people's life stories and poems.

Hieroglyphs stood for the objects they showed and, later, for sounds too.

Egyptian scribe

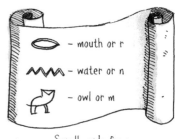

- mouth or r
- water or n
- owl or m

Scroll made from papyrus reeds

18

Writing has been found on clay seals from 2000BC in the **INDUS VALLEY**, but no one has been able to decipher it yet.

The **ANCIENT CHINESE** started writing around 1500BC, using picture symbols. This writing has been modified over the centuries, but is still in use today.

The Chinese symbol for 'tree'

The **ALPHABET** widely used today was first invented around 2000BC by people called the Phoenicians (see page 25).

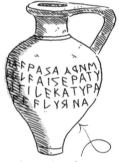

Vase with early alphabetic writing

The Rosetta Stone

CRACKING THE CODE

After the 4th century, the Egyptians stopped using hieroglyphs, and for centuries no one was able to read them. Then, in 1799 the Rosetta Stone was discovered. It was inscribed with three different scripts – hieroglyphs, another form of Egyptian writing AND Ancient Greek. Once they realized these all repeated the same text, experts were able to crack the code.

Island civilization

Europe's first civilization grew up around 2500BC, on the Mediterranean island of Crete. Its people are known as Minoans after a legendary king named Minos.

Minoan craftsmen made beautiful objects out of gold and bronze, sailors traded across the Mediterranean, and scribes used their own form of writing, known as Linear A.

Minoan snake goddess

Women played a central role in Minoan religion, which involved priestesses leading worship of goddesses.

The Minoans built many splendid palaces, but the most magnificent was at Knossos. It had over a thousand rooms, decorated with bright wall paintings, all linked by a maze of corridors to a central courtyard. There, people gathered to watch a mysterious ceremony in which acrobats somersaulted over a charging bull.

Minoan bull-leapers could be male or female.

Warrior kingdoms

On the Greek mainland, several small kingdoms developed, ruled by wealthy warrior kings in fortified cities. The people are known as Mycenaeans after the most powerful kingdom – Mycenae.

They traded with the Minoans and had a similar writing system historians call Linear B. Around 1450BC, Mycenaean warriors seized Knossos and took over Minoan sea trade. Later, they conquered the city of Troy – a real event that became a famous Greek story...

THE TROJAN HORSE
A Mycenaean king declared war on Troy after his beautiful wife, Helen, ran away with a Trojan prince.

THIS MEANS WAR!

For ten years, the Mycenaeans held Troy under siege. Then, one day they pretended to sail away, leaving a large wooden horse. The Trojans took it in, thinking it was a peace offering, but that night...

CHARGE!

We've been tricked!

...Mycenaean soldiers climbed out of the horse, fought the Trojans and won the war.

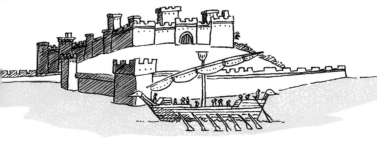

Canaanite
trade ships

Canaan

At the eastern end of the Mediterranean Sea lay the land of Canaan. It formed a vital trade link between Egypt and Mesopotamia, and changed hands many times as rulers fought bitterly for its control.

The Canaanites were expert shipbuilders and sailors. Their coastal cities became bustling trade ports, where local craftworkers made gold objects and ivory carvings that merchants sold far and wide. They also exported cedarwood – a valuable building material – from forests that grew in what is now Lebanon.

Desert people

Tribes of nomads lived on the fringes of the deserts east of Canaan. They grazed sheep and goats, settling where they could. One group reached as far as Egypt, where they were called *Habiru*, or Hebrews. Around 1250BC, they arrived in Canaan.

Unlike most people in ancient times, the Hebrews didn't worship many gods, only one. They believed their God had promised them a land where they could settle, and Canaan was that 'Promised Land'.

Sea Peoples' warships

Sea People

Around 1995BC, tribes known as the Sea People came from across the Aegean Sea. They defeated many kingdoms in the Middle East, until the Egyptians won a massive sea battle against them. After that, one of those tribes settled in southern Canaan. Descendants of this tribe became known as the Philistines, and their land was named Palestine.

David vs. Goliath

The Philistines and the Hebrews fought constantly over the best land. The Hebrew tribes chose a king named Saul to lead their fight against the Philistines. One story tells of a major battle when a brave Hebrew youth named David felled the Philistines' strongest warrior, Goliath, with a stone from his sling. David went on to succeed Saul as King of the Hebrew kingdom of Israel.

Take that, Goliath!

23

King Solomon

Under the rule of David's son, Solomon, Israel grew rich, trading with people from other lands. The people of the capital city, Jerusalem, used this wealth to build a great temple dedicated to their god.

The Hebrews lived by a set of sacred laws, called the Ten Commandments. These were carved onto stone tablets kept in a box, called the Arc of the Covenant, in a gold-lined room deep inside the temple.

SOLOMON'S TEMPLE

This basin held water to purify priests and sacred objects.

The Arc of the Covenant was flanked by winged statues.

Priests burned offerings on this altar.

A divided kingdom

After Solomon died, his land was split in two – Israel in the North and Judah in the south (see opposite). Over time, Hebrew people came to be called Jews.

Purple Phoenicians

The descendents of the Canaanites made their fortune exporting an expensive purple dye, extracted from murex shellfish. It was this that later gave their land the name 'Phoenicia', which comes from the Greek for 'purple country'. The Phoenicians were the most successful traders of their day. From coastal cities with large, fortified ports, they sailed all around the Mediterranean, building new ports including Carthage on the coast of what is now Tunisia.

Murex shell

Meanwhile, power-hungry new empires were growing to the east, and from around 720BC, Israel, Judah and Phoenicia were all overrun by invaders. Turn the page to find out more...

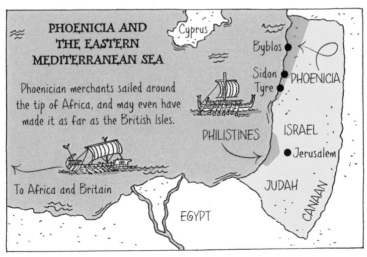

PHOENICIA AND THE EASTERN MEDITERRANEAN SEA

Phoenician merchants sailed around the tip of Africa, and may even have made it as far as the British Isles.

Cyprus

Byblos

Sidon
Tyre • PHOENICIA

PHILISTINES

ISRAEL

• Jerusalem

To Africa and Britain

JUDAH

CANAAN

EGYPT

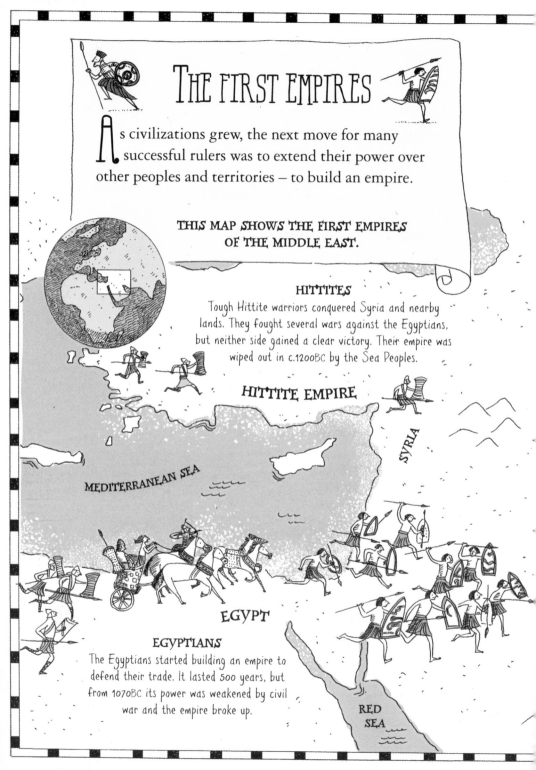

THE FIRST EMPIRES

As civilizations grew, the next move for many successful rulers was to extend their power over other peoples and territories – to build an empire.

THIS MAP SHOWS THE FIRST EMPIRES OF THE MIDDLE EAST.

HITTITES

Tough Hittite warriors conquered Syria and nearby lands. They fought several wars against the Egyptians, but neither side gained a clear victory. Their empire was wiped out in c.1200BC by the Sea Peoples.

HITTITE EMPIRE

SYRIA

MEDITERRANEAN SEA

EGYPT

EGYPTIANS

The Egyptians started building an empire to defend their trade. It lasted 500 years, but from 1070BC its power was weakened by civil war and the empire broke up.

RED SEA

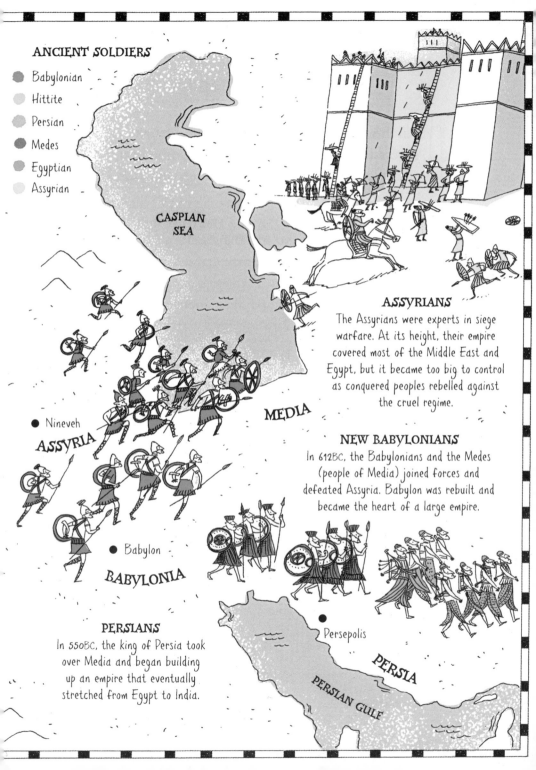

ANCIENT SOLDIERS

- ● Babylonian
- ● Hittite
- ● Persian
- ● Medes
- ● Egyptian
- ● Assyrian

CASPIAN SEA

MEDIA

● Nineveh

ASSYRIA

● Babylon

BABYLONIA

● Persepolis

PERSIA

PERSIAN GULF

ASSYRIANS

The Assyrians were experts in siege warfare. At its height, their empire covered most of the Middle East and Egypt, but it became too big to control as conquered peoples rebelled against the cruel regime.

NEW BABYLONIANS

In 612BC, the Babylonians and the Medes (people of Media) joined forces and defeated Assyria. Babylon was rebuilt and became the heart of a large empire.

PERSIANS

In 550BC, the king of Persia took over Media and began building up an empire that eventually stretched from Egypt to India.

The riches of empire

Life in the early empires of Assyria, Babylon and Persia wasn't all about battles and bloodshed. Acquiring an empire made the conquerors very rich. They seized loot and slaves, and imposed taxes on the people they conquered.

With this newfound wealth, they built magnificent cities with beautiful palaces, temples and tombs. They also kept vast libraries filled with government accounts, records of events and ideas about religion, medicine, mathematics, astrology and astronomy.

The gateways into the city of Babylon were covered with glazed blue tiles. This one was named after Ishtar, the main goddess of the city.

Babylon was a wealthy trading city filled with exotic gardens, wide streets, waterways and beautiful houses.

Persia

For Darius I, who ruled Persia from 522BC, the key to an empire's success was organization. He divided his empire into 20 provinces and appointed a governor called a satrap to run each one. He also built thousands of miles of roads, so his soldiers and messengers could travel quickly all over the empire.

People conquered by the Persians were allowed to keep their own religions and customs, as long as they obeyed Persian laws and paid their taxes. This usually kept them happy – and made Darius fabulously wealthy. However, in 513BC he invaded Greece, sparking a series of costly wars that ended in Persian defeat.

Classical Greece

In the 6th century BC, Greece was made up of several rival city-states, including Sparta, Corinth and Athens. They came together to fight the Persians, and eventually won.

Many historians refer to Greek history between 510–323BC as the 'classical' period.

Despite frequent fighting between the cities, the classical period was a golden age for Greece. The Greeks built trading cities around the Mediterranean, spreading their ideas and way of life. They were great thinkers, whose ideas and achievements in literature, art, architecture and science are still influential today.

City life in Ancient Greece

The Greek city-states all had their own forms of government. Sparta was ruled by warlike kings, but people in Athens were the first to have a form of democracy – male citizens voted to choose leaders and laws. (Women and slaves had no say.)

The Greeks built elegant temples and buildings with triangular roofs held up by tall stone pillars. Public spaces were decorated with realistic statues. Men gathered in the market square, or 'agora', to discuss politics and ideas.

Thinkers, known as philosophers, asked questions about how people should behave. Scientists and mathematicians made calculations and did experiments to find out how the world worked.

Women mostly worked at home and didn't go out alone.

Men trained as athletes so they were fit to fight wars. They held regular competitions, dedicated to the gods, including the very first Olympic Games.

Goddess statue

Most cities were built around an 'acropolis', a hill with a temple at the top, where the Greeks worshipped their gods and goddesses.

Plays were written and staged as part of religious festivals.

Actors wore masks and costumes.

Chorus

GOING TO WAR

In 431BC, war broke out between Athens, Sparta and the other city-states. The war, later called the Peloponnesian War, lasted 27 years and left all of Greece weak and exhausted.

Mighty Macedonians

To the east of Greece, King Philip II of Macedonia watched the Greeks fighting among themselves and took the opportunity to invade. By 338BC, he had conquered all of Greece. He planned to conquer the Persians next, but died too soon, leaving his son, Alexander, to put his plan into action.

Alexander was a tough soldier and a clever commander, with ambitions even greater than his father's. He led his conquering army on an expedition of over 32,000km (20,000 miles), to build the largest empire of the ancient world, taking in Syria, Egypt and the Indus Valley as well as Persia. Wherever they went, they set up Greek-style cities, many named after Alexander, spreading Greek language and culture.

I would rather live a short life of glory than a long one of obscurity.

Alexander even named one of his cities in India after his dark stallion, Bucephalus.

On the journey home from India, Alexander caught a fever. He died in Babylon in 323BC, at age 33. His name has gone down in history as Alexander the Great.

Alexander's influence

After he died, three of Alexander's generals fought for control of the empire, and it was split between them. One of them, Ptolemy, became King of Egypt, where his family ruled as pharaohs for 300 years.

Alexandria became Egypt's capital city, with a sky-scraping lighthouse, the Pharos, and a school containing a vast library, called the Musaeum. Scholars from far and wide gathered there to discuss ideas and conduct scientific experiments. The city's merchants sailed to the Black Sea and to India, bringing back spices, pearls and jewels, and silk from China.

The rise of China

By the time the Chinese were exporting their silk to the west, they had been weaving it for well over 2,000 years. They worshipped their ancestors, had a sophisticated writing system and their own distinctive art, architecture, literature, medicine and science.

The Chinese were becoming one of the greatest civilizations of ancient times...

Chinese civilization

To begin with, separate states grew up in China, ruled by powerful families, or dynasties. In 221BC, the were all brought under the rule of one emperor – and it has been a single country ever since.

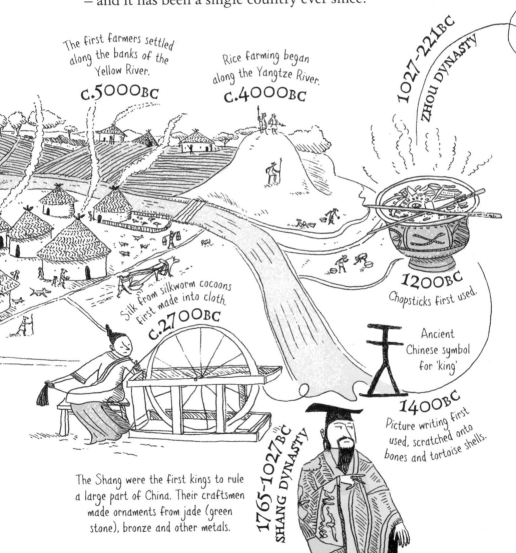

The first farmers settled along the banks of the Yellow River.
c.5000BC

Rice farming began along the Yangtze River.
c.4000BC

1027–221BC ZHOU DYNASTY

1200BC
Chopsticks first used.

Silk from silkworm cocoons first made into cloth.
c.2700BC

Ancient Chinese symbol for 'king'

1400BC
Picture writing first used, scratched onto bones and tortoise shells.

1765–1027BC SHANG DYNASTY

The Shang were the first kings to rule a large part of China. Their craftsmen made ornaments from jade (green stone), bronze and other metals.

551–479BC

A great thinker named Confucius taught that people should respect their elders and that rulers should be kind to their subjects.

481–221BC

A time of war between rival states, won by the king of the Qin state.

221–210BC
QIN SHI HUANGDI

The Qin king became the first emperor of all China. He built roads and canals and introduced standard money, weights and measures.

Shi Huangdi was buried in a huge tomb, guarded by over 7,500 life-size terracotta clay soldiers.

Building the Great Wall of China to keep out attackers began under Shi Huangdi.

FROM 200BC

Tea was farmed and drunk.

202BC–AD220
HAN DYNASTY

The Han built elegant cities, run by officials who followed the teachings of Confucius.

FROM 105BC

Chinese traders started to travel west to sell silk. Their route became known as the Silk Road, though it was really a network of several roads and trails.

Early Americans

People probably first arrived in North America during the Ice Age, when they were able to walk across an ice road from Asia to Alaska. Spreading south, settling everywhere from the frozen lands of the north, to the grassy plains, hot deserts and dizzying heights of the Andes mountains, these early Americas adopted very different ways of life depending on their environment.

While many continued to live as hunter-gatherers, groups in Central and South America seem to have been the first to take to farming. They grew potatoes, tomatoes, corn, peppers and squashes, and they kept llamas for wool, meat and milk.

The first civilizations

Around 1200BC, the first civilizations appeared. West of the Andes, people known as the Chavín made gold ornaments and built temples filled with statues of animal-like gods.

The Olmec people, who settled near the Gulf of Mexico, carved colossal heads, possibly of their rulers, from basalt boulders up to 3m (10ft) high. As part of political and religious ceremonies, they played a ball game that involved players using their hips to keep a heavy rubber ball in the air. Olmec civilization came to an end around 400BC, but some of their traditions were passed on to those who came after them.

Rainforest civilization

Deep in the Central American rainforest, the Maya people developed a rich culture. They had their own writing and an accurate calendar based on their observations of the stars and planets.

Around 300BC, they began building cities with stepped ziggurat-style buildings, palaces and temples rising above the tree canopy. These were arranged around wide plazas and ball courts, where priests oversaw a ball game similar to that of the Olmecs.

This is a carving from a ball court. In the middle, a ball player wears an elaborate headdress and a padded belt around his hips. Around the outside are Maya picture writing and numbers.

Mayan public buildings were covered with carved images of warrior kings and rain, earth, plant and animal gods. Their kings were often at war, timing battles according to dates they believed would bring them luck, and launching raids on rival cities to capture prisoners to sacrifice to the gods.

Ancient Religions

The course of history has often been determined by religion. Early societies worshipped their own local gods, as people tried to make sense of their place in the world. But a few religions spread further afield – four of the world's major faiths today took shape in ancient times.

HINDUISM

From 1500BC, priests in India chanted poems dedicated to many gods, setting out ways to live a good life. These were written down in holy books, called *Vedas*, that form the basis of Hinduism.

Vishnu, one of the principle Hindu gods, sitting on a lotus flower

BUDDHISM

In the 5th or 4th century BC, a Hindu prince named Siddhartha Gautama became so disturbed by the suffering of ordinary people that he gave up his wealth to spend his life meditating and teaching. He became known as the Buddha, or 'enlightened one', and his ideas spread through Central and East Asia.

Siddhartha is said to have reached 'enlightenment' while meditating under a tree.

38

An Indian empire

After early civilization came to an end in the Indus Valley, new tribes, the Aryans, arrived. Gradually, they spread out across northern India, where they set up lots of small kingdoms and developed a strict social pecking order called the 'caste' system.

THE 'CASTE' SYSTEM

1. At the top of the caste system were priests, scholars, kings and warriors.
2. Below them were skilled workers, merchants and officials.
3. At the bottom were the unskilled workers.

4. People who did dirty jobs were considered the lowest of the low – outside the caste system altogether.

In 324BC, a great Indian warrior named Chandragupta Maurya raised a formidable army. Fighting with war elephants, he drove out the Macedonians – who had occupied the Indus Valley under Alexander – and went on to conquer many Indian kingdoms, creating what became known as the Mauryan Empire.

JUDAISM

The Hebrew people, or Jews, believed in only one God, who would look after them if they obeyed Him. Hebrew writings, known to many as the Old Testament, describe their history and how their God appeared to prophets to pass on his laws and promises.

In the 1st century BC, the Romans conquered the Jews, eventually forcing them to flee across the Middle East and Europe.

CHRISTIANITY

Around AD27 (see below), a Jew from Nazareth, named Jesus, began preaching and gained a large following. Jewish leaders and Roman authorities saw him as a troublemaker, so they had him crucified – nailed to a cross to die.

Jesus's followers called him Christ. They wrote accounts of his life and teachings, called the Gospels, and set out to spread the Christian religion.

AD DATES

Dates immediately after the birth of Jesus are shown with the letters 'AD'. This stands for *Anno Domini*, Latin for 'in the year of the Lord'. The year after 1BC is AD1, although historians now believe Jesus was born up to seven years earlier.

Trading nations

In Africa, two kingdoms grew particularly powerful – Kush to the south of Egypt, and Axum on the Red Sea coast. Kushite kings even conquered and ruled the Egyptians for a time.

Ports sprang up by the Red Sea in Axum, and in kingdoms called Sabaea and Nabatea in Arabia. Traders in these ports grew wealthy dealing with merchants who sailed between India, Africa and the Roman Empire (see pages 49-51). They stopped along the way with rich cargoes of African ivory, gold and precious stones, Indian spices and cotton and sweet-smelling incense from Arabia.

A Bible story tells how the Queen of Sheba (probably Sabea) visited Jerusalem with rich gifts for King Solomon.

Outside the empires

While civilizations and empires rose in some places, people elsewhere – Eskimos in North America, bushmen in South America and Australia, Goths, Visigoths, Samatians and Huns in central Europe, most Africans south of the Sahara, Mongols and Scythians in central Asia – continued to live as nomadic herders.

Those on the borders of wealthy empires profited by trading with them, and sometimes by raiding them for loot. In particular, the Mongols made frequent and ferocious attacks along the Great Wall of China.

Celts

People known as the Celts lived in small farming communities across most of western Europe. They were made up of tribes that all spoke similar languages and led a similar way of life. Warrior chiefs built hilltop settlements to show how rich and powerful they were, surrounded by huge mounds and ditches to protect them from attackers and rival tribes.

The Celts developed a rich culture. Bards composed poems which they recited from memory, while craftworkers wove patterned cloth from wool and made fine bronze and gold objects decorated with swirling designs of spirals and knots.

Brooch made by a Celtic metalworker in France c.500BC

Etruscans and Latins

Further south, what is now Italy was made up of different groups of people, including Etruscans and Latins. The Etruscans grew rich trading with the Celts and the Greeks, and came to rule most of northern Italy. The Latins set up farming villages that eventually merged to become the city of Rome.

For a time, Rome had an Etruscan king. But in 509BC, its people, the Romans, rebelled and seized control. From then on, Roman power was on the rise...

42

The Roman Republic

After driving out the king, the Romans set themselves up as a republic – a state without a king. They built up a highly trained army, and went on to conquer all of Italy. From there, they spread out, gaining more and more territory.

A Roman foot soldier, or legionary

Ruling Rome

Rome was ruled by an elected council, or senate, with two leaders called consuls who were voted in each year. But as they conquered more lands, senators argued over how things should be run. Civil wars broke out as army generals and rival groups of senators fought for power.

THE CAESARS

In 49BC, a general named Julius Caesar overthrew the senate. He ruled for five years, but was stabbed to death. Rome was plunged into another civil war, until 31BC, when Caesar's heir, Octavian, took control and restored peace. Four years later, he renamed himself Emperor Caesar Augustus.

Senators were men from noble families. Later, non-nobles from rich families could be elected too.

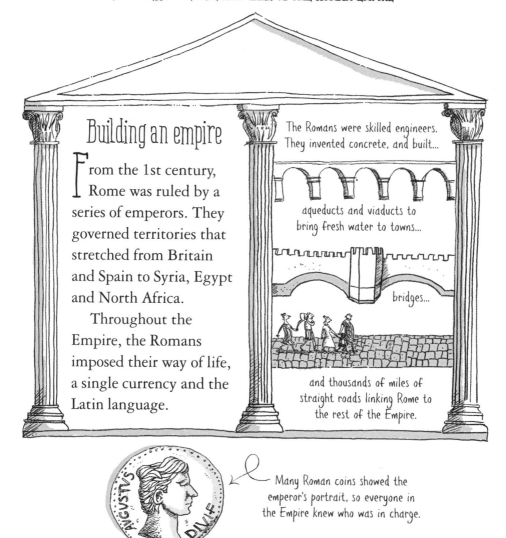

Building an empire

From the 1st century, Rome was ruled by a series of emperors. They governed territories that stretched from Britain and Spain to Syria, Egypt and North Africa.

Throughout the Empire, the Romans imposed their way of life, a single currency and the Latin language.

The Romans were skilled engineers. They invented concrete, and built...

aqueducts and viaducts to bring fresh water to towns...

bridges...

and thousands of miles of straight roads linking Rome to the rest of the Empire.

Many Roman coins showed the emperor's portrait, so everyone in the Empire knew who was in charge.

Everywhere they conquered, the Romans built new towns. These had temples, public bath houses and games arenas, including racetracks called circuses, where crowds flocked to watch the sport of chariot racing.

Turning to Christianity

As long as they paid their taxes, obeyed the law and respected the official Roman gods, people in the empire were free to worship their own gods. They were also expected to worship the emperor, but Jews and Christians believed in only one God, so refused. As a result, many faced savage persecution.

Despite this, Christianity spread through the empire. In 312, an emperor named Constantine made the religion legal, later becoming a Christian himself.

The fall of Rome

By the 3rd century, the Empire was under frequent attack from tribes outside – known to the Romans as 'barbarians'. Emperors increased taxes to pay for larger armies, even including recruits from barbarian tribes. In 284, the emperor decided the Empire was too big to manage, so he split it in two. The west was ruled from Rome and the east from Byzantium, which was renamed Constantinople by Constantine.

In 410, the city of Rome was overrun by Germanic warriors called Visigoths, then in 455 it was attacked and destroyed by another tribe, the Vandals. In the west, the power of Rome collapsed completely in 476, but in the east, the Byzantine Empire would last for another 1,000 years.

DATE CHART: THE ANCIENT WORLD

DATES	AFRICA	THE MIDDLE EAST	AMERICAS
3000BC	**3100BC:** Ancient Egypt was first united as a single kingdom by King Menes	**3500-2000BC:** The Sumerians built the first cities and were the first to invent writing.	
2500BC	**2530BC:** The Egyptians started building the Great Pyramid at Giza.	**2350-2150BC:** Akkadian Empire in Mesopotamia	
2000BC		**2000-1200BC:** Hittites **1792-1595BC:** Babylonian Empire **1600-550BC:** New Babylonians **FROM 1600BC:** Canaanites	
1500BC		**1250BC:** Hebrews settled in Canaan. Their faith became known as Judaism.	**1200-300BC:** Olmec and Chavín civilizations. Based near the Gulf of Mexico, the Olmecs
1000BC	**814BC:** Carthage built by the Phoenicians.	**1200-1000BC:** Phoenicians **1150BC:** Philistines **1000-600BC:** Assyrian Empire	carved monumental stone heads. The Chavín lived in the Andes, and were the first people in America to make objects out of gold.
500BC			
1BC **AD1**	**332BC:** Alexander the Great conquered Egypt. **30BC:** The Romans conquered Egypt.	**600-300BC:** Persian Empire **7/2BC-AD30/33** Life of Jesus of Nazareth	**FROM 300BC:** The Maya started building cities and monuments in Central America.

ASIA	AUSTRALASIA	EUROPE
3500BC: Farmers first settled in the Indus Valley.	People known as Aboriginals first settled in Australia during the Ice Age, 40,000–60,000 years ago.	FROM 3200BC: People in northern Europe started building stone circles.
2500-1800BC: Civilization in the Indus Valley		2500-1500BC: Minoan civilization on Crete.
1765-1027BC: The Shang dynasty was the first line of kings to rule much of China.		
BY 1500BC: Aryan settlers arrived in India. Their ideas formed the basis of Hinduism.	1500BC: People began settling in islands in the Pacific Ocean.	1600-1200BC: Mycenaean civilization in Greece
566/490-486/410BC: Buddha Siddhartha Guatama founded a new faith.	551-479BC: Life of Confucius	800-509BC: Etruscans 800BC-50CE: Tribes of Celts lived all over northern Europe. 510-323BC: Classical Greece
321-185BC: Mauryan Empire ruled much of India.	202BC-AD220: Han dynasty ruled in China.	356-323BC: Alexander the Great 509BC-27BC: The Roman Republic 27BC-AD476: The Roman Empire

PART TWO

THE MEDIEVAL WORLD

From the 450s

THE TIME IN THE MIDDLE

From the 14th century, European historians looked back at Classical Greece and Rome as a golden age of civilization and human achievement. They called the time after the fall of these empires 'the Middle Ages', dismissing this era as often less sophisticated.

Of course, changes in lifestyle and culture didn't stop during the Middle Ages. New kingdoms came to power in Europe, great empires rose in Africa, Asia and the Americas, and in Arabia, a powerful new religion was born – Islam.

Worlds collide

At this time, the empires and kingdoms in different parts of the world didn't have much contact with one another. But along routes such as the Silk Road, taken by merchants, nomads and pilgrims, cities grew up at trading posts, watering holes and crossroads.

These became places where people from diverse cultures came together to exchange goods and share ideas – and sometimes spread diseases and conflict too.

The word Medieval comes from *medium aevum* – the Latin for 'Middle Ages'.

After the fall of Rome

By the 5th century, the Roman Empire had split into two. The western part was invaded by barbarian tribes and a patchwork of small kingdoms formed, as the invaders settled. They brought their own religions with them, so the Christian Church went into decline in all but a few places.

Many Roman cities were destroyed in wars between the new states. Warlords began to carve out their own kingdoms, gaining power as people were forced to seek their protection during the fighting.

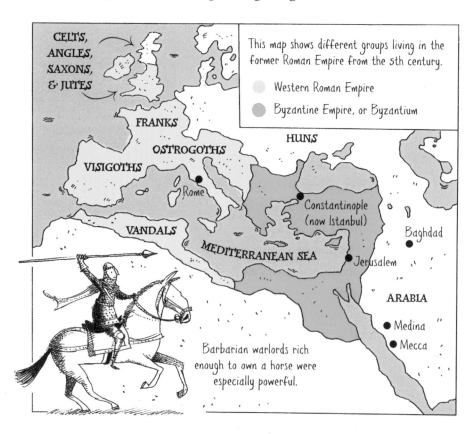

CELTS, ANGLES, SAXONS, & JUTES

This map shows different groups living in the former Roman Empire from the 5th century.

○ Western Roman Empire

● Byzantine Empire, or Byzantium

FRANKS

HUNS

OSTROGOTHS

VISIGOTHS

Rome

Constantinople (now Istanbul)

Baghdad

VANDALS

MEDITERRANEAN SEA

Jerusalem

ARABIA

Medina

Mecca

Barbarian warlords rich enough to own a horse were especially powerful.

Byzantine riches

In the east, the Roman way of life continued in the Byzantine Empire. In the 6th century, it was ruled by a mighty emperor, Justinian, who won back parts of the Western Roman Empire: southern Spain, North Africa and Italy.

Justinian had many beautiful new churches built, decorated inside with glittering mosaics. The Byzantine capital, Constantinople, was filled with merchants, artists, priests and scholars, many of whom enjoyed a life of luxury.

Emperor Justinian ruled with the help of his wife, Empress Theodora.

A new faith

Further east, the inhospitable deserts and mountains of Arabia were sparsely populated by Bedouin people – nomadic herders who worshipped many gods. But near oases and ports, busy towns had sprung up. One of these was Mecca, where locals did business with traders from the Byzantine Empire, India and East Africa. Among them were Jews and Christians who spoke of their one God.

It was in Mecca that a merchant named Muhammad announced that he had received revelations about the one true God. In 610, he started preaching.

The rise of Islam

Muhammad's message was that people must submit to one God, Allah. If they led a good life, they would be rewarded in Paradise. His teachings were written in a book called the *Koran*, the religion became known as Islam, and its followers Muslims. Muhammad's teachings angered Mecca's wealthy merchants, who drove him from the city. In 622, he escaped to Medina – this date is now counted as the first year of the Muslim calendar.

Muslims on a Haj, a religious journey, to Mecca, Islam's main holy city.

The Muslim world

The new religion spread. By the time Muhammad died in 632, most people in Arabia followed Islam. After Muhammad, the head of Islam was a spiritual and political leader called the caliph, but disagreement over who should be caliph led Islam to split into two branches – Sunnis and Shi'as. The caliphs fought wars to spread Islam, and quickly conquered an empire covering the Middle East, Egypt and North Africa, as well as a large swathes of Spain.

A golden age

Under the caliphs, a rich culture developed. Their cities were filled with mosques, schools, palaces and bathhouses. Scholars studied everything from religion and law to science. They filled libraries with books from Greece and Rome, Persia, India and China, translating them into Arabic and writing many more of their own.

GEOGRAPHERS
made maps of the routes taken by Arab explorers and merchants, who sailed to China, India and Africa.

DOCTORS
studied anatomy, surgery and diseases, as well as how to make drugs using plants and chemicals.

ASTRONOMERS
built observatories and used instruments, such as this astrolabe, to help sailors navigate by looking at the stars.

MATHEMATICIANS
developed the system of numbers we use today.

A Christian split

While Islam was on the rise, Christians in the Byzantine Empire began to develop their own distinct styles of church buildings and different ways of doing things compared to those in western Europe.

The Byzantine Church, which later became the 'Orthodox Church', was run by religious leaders called patriarchs, who held services in Greek, the official language of the Byzantine Empire.

Meanwhile, in western Europe, in what later became the 'Roman Catholic Church', priests conducted services in Latin and looked after local parishes overseen by bishops and archbishops. Ruling over them all was the Pope, based in Rome.

Spreading the word

Most rulers in western Europe could not read or write, nor did they believe in Christ. But from the end of the 6th century, the Pope sent out missionaries to teach people about Christianity and to convert their rulers. Churches and monasteries were built all over Europe and Christianity regained the strength it had lost after the fall of Rome.

Irish monks put up carved stone crosses outside their monasteries.

MONKS AND BOOKS

Some men and women dedicated their lives to God. They lived in monasteries and nunneries, religious communities where they spent their days in prayer, study and work. An important part of their work was looking after holy books and making copies of them.

These books were written out by hand. Unlike the Chinese and the Arabs, Europeans had not yet learned how to make paper, so pages were made from stretched animal hide instead. Many were beautifully illustrated and could take as long as two years to make.

Great rulers

Historians have given the title 'Great' to two Christian rulers in Europe during the 9th century – Charles, or Charlemagne, King of the Franks, and the English King Alfred of Wessex. Both improved life in their realms: they made their governments more efficient, encouraged learning, built towns and promoted trade.

Both were great warriors, too. Charlemagne conquered land in Italy and what is now Germany. In 800, the Pope crowned him 'Holy Roman Emperor'. Alfred built up his army and saved his kingdom from conquest by the Vikings (see page 56). His descendents went on to unite all of England under their rule.

Viking raiders

From the 790s, boatloads of people we now call Vikings left their homes in Denmark, Norway and Sweden in search of wealth and land.

The first to set sail were fearsome warriors in swift warships called longships. They launched smash and grab raids on monasteries and coastal villages in northern Europe, seizing loot, food, women and slaves before sailing home again.

Later, Vikings set sail to settle in new places – sometimes peacefully, sometimes by conquest.

Longships were designed to be sturdy enough to withstand rough seas, but shallow enough to sail up rivers.

Villagers, settlers and explorers

Most Vikings lived in small villages, as farmers and fishermen, metalworkers and shipbuilders. But there wasn't enough land for them all to farm, so they set sail for new lands. During the 9th and 10th centuries, Vikings settled in parts of Britain, Ireland and France, Iceland and Russia. Intrepid traders reached Constantinople and Baghdad, while explorers sailed as far as Greenland and the east coast of America.

Norman conquerors

Around the year 900, a group of Vikings, later known as the Normans, settled in northern France. They went on to conquer Sicily and parts of Italy. In 1066, a Norman duke named William invaded England. He defeated the English army in a devastating battle near Hastings and was crowned King of England. He has become famous as William the Conqueror.

A new order

To repel the Vikings, rulers in northern Europe built wooden castles along the coast as bases for rapid response units of mounted soldiers. These grew to become great stone castles manned by knights. With them a new way of life took shape that historians call the Feudal System...

European Society

Under the Feudal System, kings owned all the land, but handed out large estates to nobles in return for military services. On similar terms, nobles then gave small estates, or manors, to their knights.

The vast majority of people were lowly peasant farmers. Some were 'freemen' who owned their own farms, but most were 'serfs' who were tied to the lord's estate, having to work on his farm as well as their own while also paying him rent.

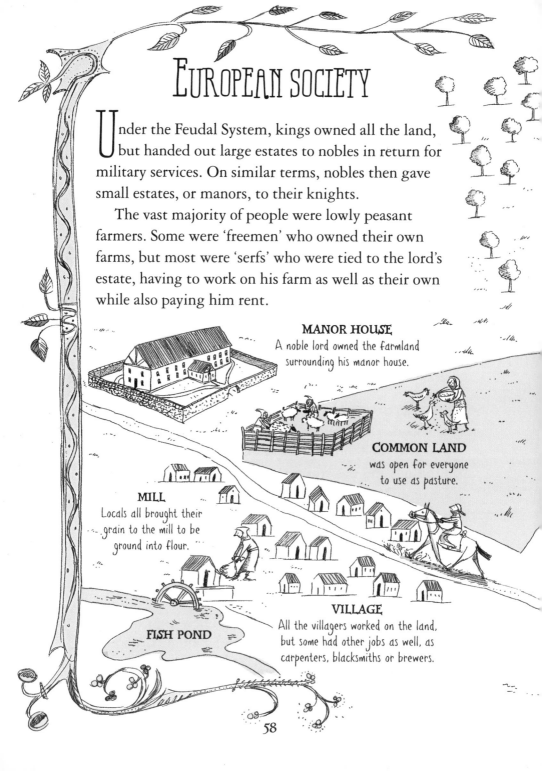

MANOR HOUSE
A noble lord owned the farmland surrounding his manor house.

COMMON LAND
was open for everyone to use as pasture.

MILL
Locals all brought their grain to the mill to be ground into flour.

VILLAGE
All the villagers worked on the land, but some had other jobs as well, as carpenters, blacksmiths or brewers.

FISH POND

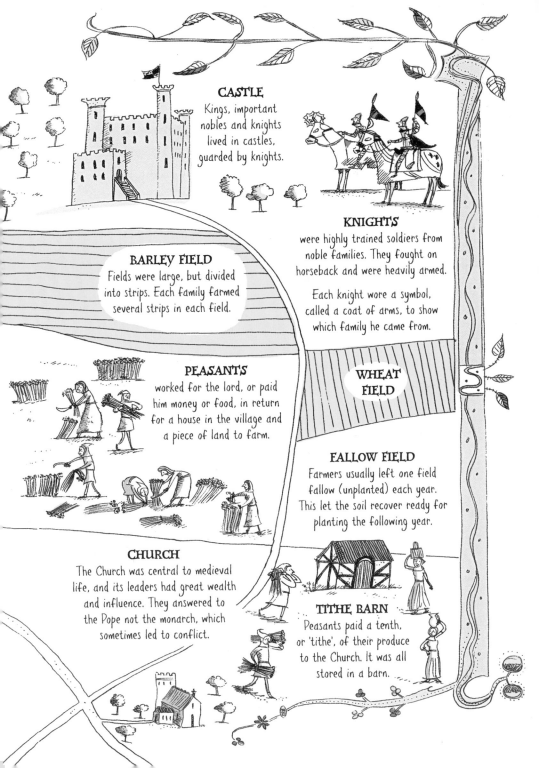

CASTLE
Kings, important nobles and knights lived in castles, guarded by knights.

KNIGHTS
were highly trained soldiers from noble families. They fought on horseback and were heavily armed.

Each knight wore a symbol, called a coat of arms, to show which family he came from.

BARLEY FIELD
Fields were large, but divided into strips. Each family farmed several strips in each field.

PEASANTS
worked for the lord, or paid him money or food, in return for a house in the village and a piece of land to farm.

WHEAT FIELD

FALLOW FIELD
Farmers usually left one field fallow (unplanted) each year. This let the soil recover ready for planting the following year.

CHURCH
The Church was central to medieval life, and its leaders had great wealth and influence. They answered to the Pope not the monarch, which sometimes led to conflict.

TITHE BARN
Peasants paid a tenth, or 'tithe', of their produce to the Church. It was all stored in a barn.

Tough at the top

The Medieval period was time of turbulence and frequent wars. Most often, battles raged between rival kings competing for territory. But if a king was weak or unpopular, his own nobles might fight each other in private feuds, or even turn against him. On top of all that, civil wars could break out whenever rival claimants fought for kingship.

To protect themselves against attacks, kings and nobles built stone castles surrounded by strong, high walls. Much of a king's strength lay in his ability to raise enough taxes from his people to pay for all the fighting, and to call up a large army of loyal knights, whenever he needed to go to war.

A KNIGHT IN TRAINING

It took ten years of training to become a knight.
Only sons of wealthy nobles could do it, because horses were very expensive.

Arise, Sir Percy!

PAGE BOY
A boy started his training by being sent to a noble's house as a page. He did odd jobs, learned to ride and how to fight.

SQUIRE
When he was older, he became a squire. He looked after a knight's horse and equipment, and went with him into battle.

KNIGHT
If he proved he had the skill and the courage, the young man would be 'knighted' by a noble or even a king.

Power struggles

The Church owned lots of land, and bishops often became kings' ministers. This led to bitter disputes over the rights of kings to raise taxes from Church lands, how much say kings had in the appointment of bishops, and how much influence popes had over a king's government.

It could be dangerous for a king to ignore his nobles. In England, in 1215, King John's nobles forced him to sign *Magna Carta*, an agreement limiting his power and giving them a say in government. In the reign of his son, Henry III, a council of nobles and bishops was set up to help the king make decisions. This was the beginnings of England's first parliament.

Religious wars

Conflict grew between European rulers and the Muslim Empire, because the Muslims captured lands once held by the Byzantines – including Jerusalem. In 1095 the Pope called for Christian soldiers to join a religious war, or Crusade, to claim back what they called the Holy Land – Jerusalem and Palestine.

At first, the Crusaders succeeded. They set up a Christian kingdom called Outremer, but the Muslims retaliated, and by 1291 they had taken back the region.

The Crusades cost thousands of lives, and conflict in the Holy Land continued long after.

Towns and guilds

Towns started to grow all over Europe during the Middle Ages. They were usually built near a castle, and townspeople paid rent to the lord of the castle instead of working for him.

Craftworkers set up workshops where they made everything from clothes to pots and pans. Others worked as bakers, brewers, blacksmiths, doctors and innkeepers. To make sure goods were of high quality, and that prices and wages were fair, workers in each trade or craft got together to form societies called guilds. These could become rich and influential. Most towns were run by a mayor, who would be chosen from among the most important members of the guilds.

As towns grew wealthier, some places bought a document from the local lord or king, called a charter, granting them independence. Great independent cities, such as Venice, even set up their own rulers and their own laws.

Merchants and bankers

After the Crusades, knights came home with new ideas from Islamic literature and science, and with a taste for goods from the East, such as spices, dried fruits, sugar and luxury fabrics.

Some merchants began trading imported luxuries for local goods and raw materials, both at home and abroad. To fund trading expeditions, they borrowed money from rich Italian merchants who set up banks with branches across Europe from the 14th century.

Terrible plague and revolting peasants

In 1346 a plague, the Black Death, swept out of Asia, possibly brought on trade ships returning to Italy from the East. It spread rapidly through Europe, killing about half the population.

The devastating effects of the plague, wars, taxes, high prices and low wages led many peasants and poorer townspeople to revolt. They were often savagely cut down, but in some places, wages eventually became fairer and serfs were freed. It was the beginning of the end of the Feudal System.

63

Asian rulers

In Asia, new kingdoms and empires were taking shape. Traders and monks trekked thousands of miles, spreading new customs and ideas across the continent, and nomadic Mongol warriors wreaked terror as they invaded and seized control of great swathes of land.

A golden age in China

After the Han dynasty ended in the 3rd century, China suffered a long period of instability, as power changed hands between weak emperors and ambitious army generals. Eventually, a strong dynasty, the Sui, restored peace. They were followed by the Tang, then the Song. It was a golden age of Chinese achievement:

SUI: 581-618
Built a network of canals, making it easier for merchants to travel around China.

Introduced standard coins throughout.

Encouraged Buddhism to spread.

Further developed the civil service.

TANG: 618-907
Expanded the army and conquered lands from Korea in the east and Turkestan in the west.

Poets and artists produced great works.

Developed fine porcelain pottery, or china.

Used wooden blocks to print books on paper.

SONG: 960-1279
The first government to set up a permanent navy for military and trading expeditions.

The first to find true north using a compass.

The first to issue bank notes.

Gunpowder was invented and used for fireworks.

Mongol hordes

The wide, treeless plains between China and eastern Europe were home to the Mongols – nomadic tribes, who lived in tents called yurts and roamed the land looking for fresh pasture and raiding rival tribes.

Mongol warriors were expert horsemen and ruthless fighters. Chief among them was a man named Temujin, who amassed a horde of 20,000 warriors, and brought the other Mongol tribes under his rule. In 1206, they proclaimed him 'Genghis Khan', meaning 'supreme ruler'. Led by Genghis, the Mongols invaded northern China, killing thousands as they went.

By 1279, Kublai Khan, grandson of Genghis, had conquered all of China. He founded the Yuan dynasty, making Beijing his capital. Foreign merchants – mainly Arabs, but also a few intrepid Europeans – ventured along the Silk Road seeking their fortune trading gold and silver for Chinese silk, porcelain and carved jade.

In the 1270s-90s, Venetian merchant Marco Polo visited the court of Kublai Khan, and spent time exploring the Mongol Empire. He was even sent on diplomatic missions for the emperor.

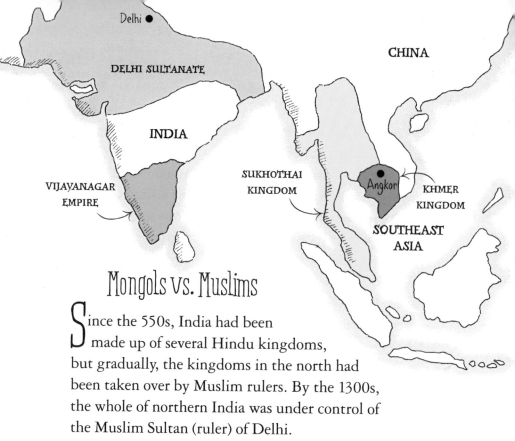

Delhi ●

CHINA

DELHI SULTANATE

INDIA

VIJAYANAGAR
EMPIRE

SUKHOTHAI
KINGDOM

Angkor

KHMER
KINGDOM

SOUTHEAST
ASIA

Mongols vs. Muslims

Since the 550s, India had been
made up of several Hindu kingdoms,
but gradually, the kingdoms in the north had
been taken over by Muslim rulers. By the 1300s,
the whole of northern India was under control of
the Muslim Sultan (ruler) of Delhi.

Then, a new Mongol leader, Tamerlane, rose to
power. He began building a new empire, grabbing
territory in Persia and Russia, and invading India.
In 1398, Tamerlane attacked and destroyed Delhi, but
the Muslims took back control soon after his death.

Strong in the south

The sultans of Delhi launched frequent attacks
against the Hindu kingdoms of southern India.
But the local rulers joined forces to form the powerful
Vijayanagar Empire, and stood their ground.

Live and let live

Hindu kings lived in luxurious palaces with hundreds of servants, as well as dancers, musicians and poets to entertain them. They built towering Hindu temples, but also let Buddhist monks teach their religion. Indian traders and monks went out across southeast Asia, helping to spread Hinduism and Buddhism.

A kingdom in the jungle

Cambodia was home to people called the Khmers. They worshipped their kings as gods, but also built huge temples to the Hindu gods. The capital, Angkor, was a splendid city of some half a million people, built around a great temple called Angkor Wat.

In 1431, Angkor was invaded by an army from the nearby Sukhothai Kingdom. By 1500, the Khmer cities had been abandoned, and were invaded instead by the jungle, as roots took a stranglehold on doorways, and creepers twisted up crumbling towers.

Angkor Wat was built as a Hindu temple, but it later became a Buddhist one.

Emperors and shoguns

By the 600s, Japan was ruled by a long-established line of emperors. The Japanese emperors of the 600s admired Chinese culture. They built Chinese-style palaces and based their arts and crafts, laws and government on Chinese ideas. Buddhism also arrived from China, soon becoming popular alongside the existing Japanese religion of Shinto.

To begin with, the emperors owned all land in Japan, but gradually, they gave away large estates to powerful noble families. In 1192, the emperor appointed a noble named Minamoto Yoritomo as military commander, or *shogun*.

Way of the warrior

From then on, the shoguns were the real rulers of Japan, keeping power with the help of local lords, the *daimyo*, and their bands of warriors, the *samurai*. Samurai were trained to die rather than surrender, and were strong enough to fight off an attempted invasion by Kublai Khan's Mongol army.

Samurai warriors fought with a long, curved sword, in a protective body suit made of leather.

Pacific People

Life at this time was very different in Australia, New Zealand and the Pacific Islands. People didn't live in cities or work the land as part of a feudal system. Most lived by fishing, hunting and gathering, though some on the Pacific Islands had taken up farming.

The Maoris in New Zealand and the people of Easter Island, way out in the middle of the Pacific Ocean, worshipped their ancestors and believed certain places were sacred. For the Australian Aboriginals, the world was created by spirits in an age called the 'Dream Time'. These customs and beliefs are still held by many in the region today.

HEI-TIKI

A hei-tiki is a greenstone ornament worn by Maoris around their necks. These are said to represent early ancestors and are passed down through the generations as family heirlooms.

BOOMERANGS

Australians used spears and curved throwing sticks called boomerangs to catch fast-moving animals such as emus and kangaroos.

MOAI

Between the years 1000 and 1500, people on Easter Island erected as many as 900 carved statues, called *moai*, all around the coast. Towering up to 12m (40ft) high, the stone figures with extra big heads are thought to represent ancient chiefs.

The Americas

Life in America continued in isolation from the rest of the world, except for a few adventurous Vikings and traders from Asia. While groups such as the Inuits and the Plains people lived as hunter-gatherers, a number of civilizations started settling and building towns.

NORTH AMERICA

INUIT PEOPLE

PLAINS PEOPLE

PUEBLO PEOPLE

MOUND BUILDERS

Cahokia

THE INUIT PEOPLE
of the icy north lived by fishing and hunting seals and walruses. In the winter, they lived in igloos – houses built from blocks of ice.

Chichén Itzá

AZTECS

Tenochtitlán

MAYA

Chan Chan

Machu Picchu

INCAS

Cuzco

PLAINS PEOPLE
planted crops in the spring and hunted buffalo in the summer. They lived in tents, called teepees, made from buffalo hide stretched over wooden frames.

SOUTH AMERICA

Mud and mounds

During the 700s, farmers started to settle, building North America's first towns. The people of the Mississippi Valley became known as 'Mound Builders' because in their towns, such as Cahokia, they built temples and homes for important people on top of huge flat-topped earth mounds.

In the deserts of the southwest, houses built from dried mud, or 'adobe', had as many as five stories, sometimes built into the sides of canyons. Settlements like this, and their people, became known as 'Pueblos'.

Llamas

Cities among the clouds

High in the Andes Mountains of South America, Inca farmers dug terraces into the mountains to grow their crops, and used llamas to carry heavy loads. They lived in stone-built towns, with temples and observatories for viewing the stars. To travel between towns, messengers, traders and soldiers used a network of roads, with rope bridges made from woven reeds.

71

The Aztec Empire

Around 1300, a tribe of nomads called the Mexica – later known as the Aztecs – arrived in what is now Mexico, from desert lands further north. On an island in Lake Texcoco, with mountains all around, they settled and founded what would become their capital city and the heart of the Aztec Empire – Tenochtitlán.

By the 1450s, Tenochtitlán was home to around 500,000 people. Modern Mexico City is now built on top of it, but Lake Texcoco no longer exists.

Aztecs didn't have money, but traders exchanged goods in the market place, and sometimes used cocoa beans as currency.

Get your lovely jade and turquoise ornaments here!

The city and smaller islands were connected to the shore by a series of causeways, canals and aqueducts bringing fresh water.

How many cocoa beans for this pot?

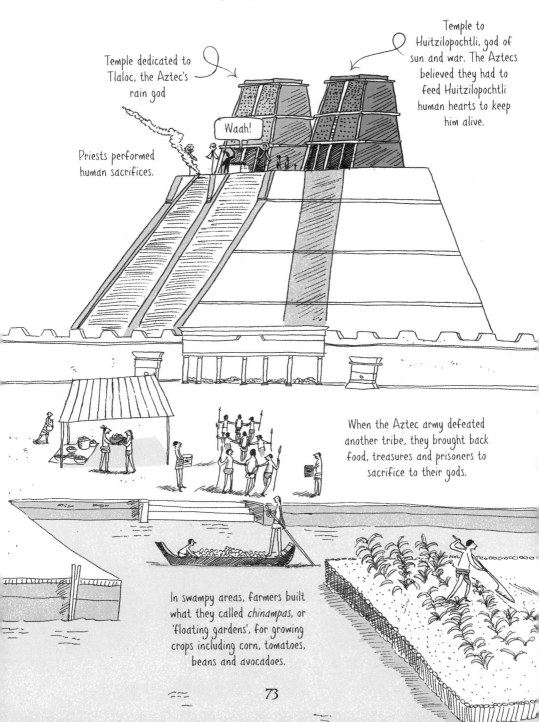

Temple dedicated to Tlaloc, the Aztec's rain god

Temple to Huitzilopochtli, god of sun and war. The Aztecs believed they had to feed Huitzilopochtli human hearts to keep him alive.

Priests performed human sacrifices.

Waah!

When the Aztec army defeated another tribe, they brought back food, treasures and prisoners to sacrifice to their gods.

In swampy areas, farmers built what they called *chinampas*, or 'floating gardens', for growing crops including corn, tomatoes, beans and avocadoes.

73

AFRICAN CITIES

By the 800s, Muslim traders from North Africa had begun to make the arduous month-long camel ride across the Sahara Desert to West Africa. The locals there grew rich trading gold, slaves and ivory for salt – essential for preserving food in the baking heat – and goods from further north. Many converted to Islam.

Gold mines were the source of fabulous wealth that helped a trading post on the Niger River to grow into the city of Timbuktu, while three rich kingdoms in the region rose and fell: Ghana, Mali, then Songhai.

THE WORLD'S RICHEST MAN...

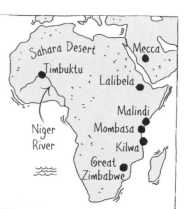

...in Medieval times was Musa Keita I, Mansa (ruler) of Mali. He was a devout Muslim, and in 1324, he went on the pilgrimage, or Haj, from West Africa to Mecca.

Sahara Desert · Mecca
Timbuktu
Lalibela
Niger River · Malindi
Mombasa
Kilwa
Great Zimbabwe

Mansa Musa's caravan of attendants, as well as camels and horses laden with gold, was said to have stretched as far as the eye could see.

Along the way, Mansa Musa built mosques and gave away gold to poor people he met on the journey.

City of mud, mosques and books

Timbuktu was one of the most cosmopolitan cities of the 1300s. It had a royal palace, bustling markets and beautiful mosques, all built from mud bricks. There was also a famous university there that attracted scholars and booksellers from across the Muslim world.

Eastern cities

Busy ports grew up along the east coast, where Africans traded with merchants from Arabia and others from as far away as China.

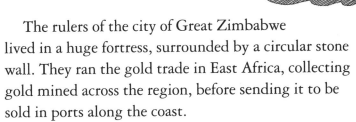

In the early 1400s, a Chinese trading expedition sailed home with a boatload of African animals for the emperor.

The rulers of the city of Great Zimbabwe lived in a huge fortress, surrounded by a circular stone wall. They ran the gold trade in East Africa, collecting gold mined across the region, before sending it to be sold in ports along the coast.

To the north was the Christian kingdom of Ethiopia. Around 1200, King Lalibela, wanted to build a holy city based on Jerusalem, so he had 11 churches hewn from the rocky hillside at a place of pilgrimage later named after him. Each church was made in the shape of a cross, and some were connected by tunnels.

75

ALL CHANGE IN THE EAST

At the start of the Middle Ages, tribes from central Asia, including Slavs, Magyars and Bulgars, had migrated west. By the 10th century, they had settled in the east of Europe, founding the states of Poland, Moravia, Bohemia (now Czechia or the Czech Republic), Croatia, Bulgaria and Hungary.

Meanwhile, Russia was established by people descended from Viking traders, known as the Rus. In 989, their ruler Vladimir I married a Byzantine princess and made Orthodox Christianity the official religion. His capital city, Kiev, became an important place of culture, religion and art.

Clash of the conquerors

Further south, in what is now Turkey, a tribe of Turks called the Seljuks gained power. They spread out, taking control of parts of the Byzantine and Muslim Empires. However, during the 13th century, the Seljuks, Russia, Poland and Hungary were all invaded by conquering Mongol armies. The Seljuks lost all of their lands, except Turkey.

Then, in 1301, an ambitious Turkish prince named Osman declared himself *Sultan* (ruler) of all the Turks. He and his successors seized land around the Black Sea and in the Balkans, building up what became known as the Ottoman Empire.

Constantinople was one of the most heavily fortified cities in the world. It finally fell in 1453, after a 53-day siege led by the Ottoman Sultan Mehmed II, who subjected the city to heavy cannonfire.

The fall of Constantinople

Over the next 150 years, the Ottomans took over more and more land from the Byzantines, until only Constantinople, defended by strong city walls, was left. The last emperor died fighting to save his city, but after a relentless siege, the Ottomans stormed in and took control. The city was later renamed Istanbul.

In the aftermath, waves of refugees, including many scholars, fled to Europe. Byzantine churches in Ottoman lands were converted into mosques, while Russia became the leading Orthodox country.

The fall of Constantinople helped to usher in what some historians call the Early Modern Age.

DATE CHART: THE MEDIEVAL WORLD

	THE AMERICAS	EUROPE
500		527-565: Reign of Justinian in the Byzantine Empire
600	c.600: Maya civilization was at is peak.	
700	c.700: Mississippi people started building towns.	
800		790s-1100s: Viking raids 800-814: Reign of Charlemagne as Holy Roman Emperor
900	c.900: Pueblo people started building adobe towns.	871-899: Reign of Alfred the Great in England
1000	c.1000: A Viking named Leif Erikson reached North America.	1054: The Christian Church in eastern Europe split permanently from the Church in western Europe.
1100		1066: Normans conquered England
1200		1215: King John of England was made to sign Magna Carta.
1300	1300s: Aztecs built an empire.	
		1340s-1350s: The Black Death...
1400	1438: Incas started building an empire.	1453: The fall of Constantinople

AFRICA	ASIA	AUSTRALASIA
490S: Vandals invaded North Africa.		
533: Byzantines conquered North Africa.	581-618: Sui dynasty in China	
	610: Muhammad started preaching Islam in Mecca.	
697: Arabs conquered North Africa.	618-907: Tang dynasty in China	
C.700: The Kingdom of Ghana was created.	FROM 632: Arab caliphs started to build a Muslim empire.	C.750: The Maoris reached New Zealand.
	802: The Khmer Kingdom was created in Cambodia.	
	960-1279: Song dynasty in China	
C.1000: The Kingdoms of Benin and Ife were founded.	1055: Seljuk Turks conquered Baghdad.	FROM 1000: People on Easter Island built stone statues.
	1095-1291: The Crusades	
1181-1221: Lalibela ruled in Ethiopia.	1192: The shoguns took control in Japan.	
1200: Kingdom of Mali was created.	1206-1227: Genghis Khan built the Mongol Empire.	
	1270S-1290S: Marco Polo visited Kublai Khan's China.	
1324: Musa Keita I's Haj	1301: Osman I made himself Sultan of the Ottoman Empire.	
	1336: Vijayanagar Empire formed in southern India.	
...started in Asia and spread to Europe and North Africa		
1350: The city of Great Zimbabwe was at its largest.	1398: Tamerlane invaded northern India.	

PART THREE

THE EARLY MODERN WORLD

From the 1450s

MAPPING THE WORLD

Five hundred years ago, vast stretches of the world were unmapped. The great empires that had grown up in the Middle Ages boasted grand cities, proud customs and religions, but most people never wandered far from their place of birth and had little idea of the vast scale and potential riches of the lands beyond their own.

Setting sail

Merchant caravans could take a year on hazardous overland trails to reach distant countries. But the sacks of spices, silks and other precious goods they traded brought fabulous wealth. When Constantinople was captured by the Ottoman Turks, the trade link between Europe and Asia was severed, prompting European rulers to seek alternative, faster routes by sea.

And so they sent navigators to scout the unknown seas. These voyages opened an era of worldwide trade and exploration that helped to shape the modern world.

THE RENAISSANCE

While navigators explored new horizons, a revolution in art, science and attitudes swept across Europe. The Renaissance, as it became known, started in Italy, where artists and writers were inspired by classical art, architecture and literature from ancient Greece and Rome to explore new ideas of their own.

Architects built beautiful new buildings with domes, pillars and rounded arches.

Renaissance artists and sculptors sketched and copied ancient statues and used real people as models to make their work look as lifelike as possible.

Ancient statue

Sculptor

Model

Master painter

Artists in training

Patrons

Wealthy patrons, including Lorenzo de' Medici from Florence, paid the best artists to create paintings and statues for them.

Some of the people who made their names in the Renaissance are still famous today:

Leonardo designed these mechanical wings, though they probably wouldn't have worked!

Leonardo da Vinci (1452–1519) was an artist, sculptor, architect and inventor. His masterpiece, the *Mona Lisa*, is one of the most famous paintings in the world.

Based in Bruges, now in Belgium, painter Jan van Eyck (c.1390–1441) was the first to become famous for using oil paints.

Michelangelo Buonarroti (1475–1564) painted the Sistine Chapel in Rome and made a marble statue of the biblical hero David.

Isabella d'Este (1474–1539) ruled the Italian state of Mantua. She was a fashion leader, diplomat, musician and patron of the arts.

Architect Andrea Palladio (1508–1580) designed palaces and churches based on the proportions of classical Greek and Roman buildings.

A revolution in science

During the Renaissance, educated people were encouraged to study a wide range of subjects, from art and literature, to politics and philosophy, mathematics and science. Inventors worked on new designs for clocks, weapons, engines, telescopes and microscopes. These enabled scientists to make new observations that gave rise to revolutionary discoveries.

Chemistry and medicine

People called alchemists tried to brew potions that would give eternal life or turn cheap metals into gold. They didn't succeed, of course, but they did invent useful apparatus and learned how to make and use different chemicals. This eventually developed into the science of chemistry.

Doctors studied plants and animals, and dissected corpses to find out more about the human body.

Anatomy students watched bodies being dissected.

Changing views

Since ancient times, most people had believed the Sun and planets revolved around the Earth. But in 1543, a Polish priest, Nikolaus Copernicus, published a book showing that the planets went around the Sun.

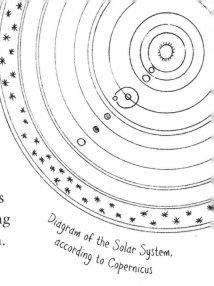

Diagram of the Solar System, according to Copernicus

Galileo

At first, people refused to believe Copernicus. But an Italian astronomer, Galileo Galilei, was able to prove him right, thanks to observations made through his newly invented telescope.

Galileo's findings caused outrage, because they went against the beliefs of the Catholic Church. In 1633, he was put on trial by the Church, who held him under house arrest for the rest of his life.

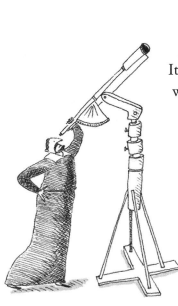

English scientist Robert Hooke was the first to describe the 'cells' that make up plant and animal tissue. He made sketches like this, based on what he discovered using recently invented microscopes.

Priests and protests

The Catholic Church was the cornerstone of everyday life across Western Europe in the 1500s. But many people were becoming unhappy with the way it was run. Some parish priests were so poorly educated they could barely say the services, which were given in Latin. Meanwhile, many high-ranking churchmen were abusing their positions to gain wealth and influence.

Reformation

In 1517, Martin Luther, a German monk and professor, wrote a list of reforms he believed the Church needed to make. He won followers across Europe, who protested against the Church, and eventually broke away from it. They earned the name 'Protestants', and the movement became known as the Reformation.

From Switzerland to Scotland, Protestants set up their own churches, where they held services in their own languages. In many places rulers adopted various forms of Protestantism as the official religion.

Luther is said to have have pinned his list, later known as the 95 Theses, to church doors in Wittenberg, in Germany, sparking wider debate.

Spreading the word

The ideas that fuelled the Reformation spread rapidly, thanks to the very latest in mass communications: the printing press, invented in the 1440s by a German bookseller named Johannes Gutenberg.

Until then, in Europe books had to be copied out by hand. Now they could be printed quickly and cheaply, in large numbers, making books, pamphlets and even translations of the Bible available to many more people in their own languages.

The first major book Gutenberg printed was the Bible.

Rome fights back

To win people back, leaders of the Catholic Church launched a series of reforms that became known as the Counter Reformation. They set up training colleges for priests and founded a new religious order, called the Society of Jesus, whose members, the Jesuits, set out to convert people back to Catholicism.

Meanwhile, the Inquisition, a system of courts run by monks in Catholic countries, tried and punished Protestants and anyone who went against their teaching, or who they considered to be a bad Catholic.

OCEAN PATHFINDERS

Craving exotic goods from the Far East, Europe's rulers in the 1400s sent explorers to find the way by sea. It soon became a race, not only to master the seas, but also to claim lands they hadn't previously known existed.

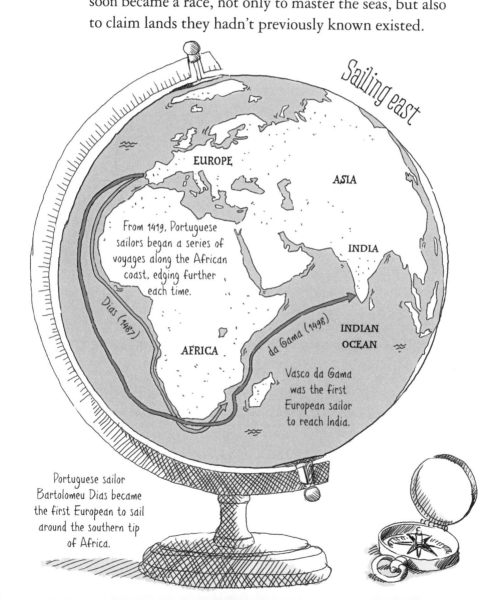

Sailing east

EUROPE

ASIA

INDIA

From 1419, Portuguese sailors began a series of voyages along the African coast, edging further each time.

Dias (1487)

da Gama (1498)

INDIAN OCEAN

AFRICA

Vasco da Gama was the first European sailor to reach India.

Portuguese sailor Bartolomeu Dias became the first European to sail around the southern tip of Africa.

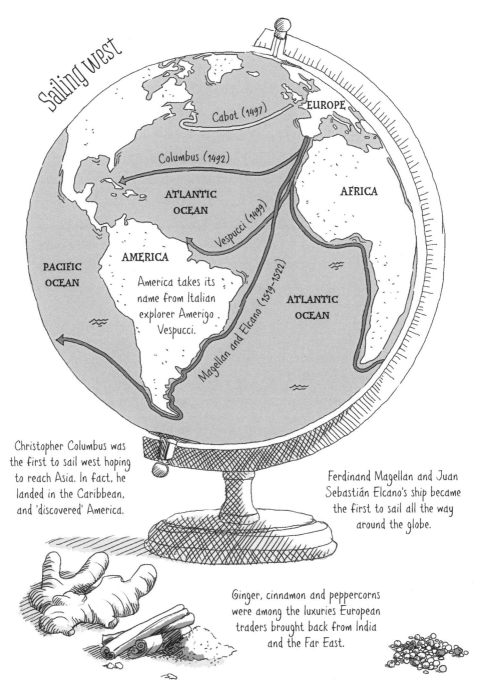

Sailing west

Cabot (1497)

EUROPE

Columbus (1492)

ATLANTIC
OCEAN

AFRICA

Vespucci (1499)

PACIFIC
OCEAN

AMERICA

America takes its
name from Italian
explorer Amerigo
Vespucci.

Magellan and Elcano (1519-1522)

ATLANTIC
OCEAN

Christopher Columbus was
the first to sail west hoping
to reach Asia. In fact, he
landed in the Caribbean,
and 'discovered' America.

Ferdinand Magellan and Juan
Sebastián Elcano's ship became
the first to sail all the way
around the globe.

Ginger, cinnamon and peppercorns
were among the luxuries European
traders brought back from India
and the Far East.

New World seekers

Spanish adventurers, known as *conquistadors*, wasted no time following Columbus to the Americas, which they called the 'New World', to seize land and exploit it for their own gain. They conquered much of the West Indies, Mexico and South America. In the process, they all but wiped out the Aztecs and Incas. Meanwhile, the Portuguese claimed territory in Brazil for their king.

In North America, the French concentrated on what is now Canada, for the profitable fur trade. English, Dutch and German colonists settled in what would later become the United States.

This picture is based on one of many vivid pictorial records the Aztecs made of the Spanish conquest.

The locals had never seen horses before, and their weapons were no match for those of the European soldiers.

Profit...

The dangers and hardships for colonists of the New World were immense, but so were the riches. As well as finding fertile farmland, in South America they discovered gold, silver and emeralds.

European colonists brought their own animals and crops with them, and sent home produce such as corn and potatoes, introducing them to Europe for the first time. In the southern parts of North America, plantation owners made huge profits growing cotton and tobacco to ship back to Europe. In the West Indies, sugar became the most lucrative crop.

...and loss

But all that came at a terrible cost. Local people were put to work on estates and in mines, where conditions were so harsh that thousands died. Thousands more succumbed to unfamiliar European diseases that their immune systems couldn't fight.

Piracy on the high seas

The Spaniards sent ships home laden with treasure, which came under frequent attack from pirates who prowled the seas, waiting to strike. French and English sailors were even rewarded by their governments for bringing back gold and silver seized from Spanish ships.

GREAT DYNASTIES

While European explorers grabbed land in the New World, their rulers jostled for power at home. By the 1500s, the Old World – Europe, Asia and the Muslim empires – was dominated by a handful of ruling families, or dynasties.

European superpowers

Through clever marriages, the Austrian ruling family, the Habsburgs, acquired power across Europe. The dynasty reached its peak under Emperor Charles V, who ruled swathes of Europe including Spain, parts of Italy, the Netherlands and the Holy Roman Empire – a collection of German and central European states.

A precarious balance

The Valois, and later the Bourbon, kings of France fought many battles with the Habsburgs, whose territories encircled France, and with whom they competed for control over several Italian states.

In England, the Tudor monarchs held the balance of power between the Habsburgs and the Valois, often siding with Spain over France. But relations with the Spanish, who were staunch Catholics, were severed when King Henry VIII broke away from the Catholic Church in Rome.

Trouble at the top

Despite enormous wealth coming into Spain from South America, constant wars against the French and the Ottomans meant Charles V was often in debt and overstretched. To add to his difficulties, as Holy Roman Emperor he ruled over many German states that became Protestant during the Reformation and resented having a Catholic ruler.

The Holy Roman Emperor's crown

Exhausted, Charles V stepped down in 1556, and divided up his lands. His brother Ferdinand ruled Austria and the Holy Roman Empire, while Philip II, Charles's son, became King of Spain, the Netherlands and Spain's New World empire.

Religious conflicts

Religious divisions after the Reformation led to nearly a century of wars between Catholics and Protestants. One of the bloodiest was a civil war that almost tore France apart. More wide-reaching was the Thirty Years' War, which started in 1618 in Bohemia, but soon drew most of Europe into a terrible war of religion. It ended with no clear victor, but with the German states, the Netherlands and Switzerland all gaining independence from the Habsburg Empire.

A new start for China

In China, the Mongol rulers of the Yuan dynasty were driven out in 1368. A new Chinese dynasty, the Ming, took control. After years of famine, poverty and unrest under Yuan rule, the Ming worked to rebuild a broken land. They improved harvests, roads and government across the empire, bringing a new age of prosperity.

Life behind walls

In the heart of the capital, Beijing, they built a huge palace complex known as the Forbidden City. Within its high walls were wide squares, gardens and imposing halls, decked with sculptures and ornate tiles. Emperors and their families lived in luxury, surrounded by an army of servants, advisors and bodyguards.

The Hall of Harmony in the Forbidden City

Soldiers

Officials

Silver for silk

The Chinese began to trade with Portuguese merchants, who first arrived in 1514. The Portuguese exchanged silver from mines in their colonies in Peru and Mexico, for silk, porcelain and tea. After the Portuguese, other Europeans were also allowed to trade, but under strict regulation. All goods had to be paid for in silver, because the Chinese merchants had little interest in buying goods from the West.

Pillagers and pirates

China faced many threats. Japanese pirates menaced coastal towns, while Mongol raiders attacked from the north, prompting Ming emperors to fortify the Great Wall. In 1556, a terrible earthquake struck, followed by a spate of natural disasters and rebellions.

In 1644, the Ming were swept aside by rulers from Manchuria, a region in the northeast of China, who set up the Manchu Qing dynasty – China's last emperors.

Ladies-in-waiting

The emperor rode in an elephant-drawn coach.

Splendid isolation

While the great age of exploration was opening up much of the world, the same wasn't true for Japan. In 1603, after decades of civil war between the country's noble landowners, the *daimyo*, a new line of shoguns from the Tokugawa clan took power.

The Tokugawa united the warring nobles and closed Japan's borders. In 1639, shogun Tokugawa Iemitsu banned foreign travel and deported all foreigners, other than a few Chinese and Dutch traders who were allowed to dock on a tiny man-made island in Nagasaki Bay. To preserve Japan's ancient culture and beliefs, Christianity was banned too.

From samurai to sumo

The Tokugawas made Edo (now Tokyo) their capital, so their rule is known as the Edo period. It was a time of peace and growth. Samurai turned from their warlike ways to become teachers, artists and local officials. Some used their combat training to help set up sumo wrestling schools and tournaments.

Tea-drinking ceremonies, first introduced from China by Buddhist monks in the 6th century, developed and became more elaborate in the Edo period.

96

Edo culture

Arts and crafts flourished during the Edo period. Artists produced prints showing everyday life, with bold outlines and delicate details. In the city, crowds flocked to see puppet shows and stylized musical dramas called *kabuki*.

Kabuki performers wore dramatic costumes and mask-like make-up.

Black ships

Japan remained locked away from the world for over two centuries. Then in 1853, four American gunships steamed into Edo Bay. Their commander, Commodore Perry, persuaded the shogun to sign a trading agreement with America.

Before long, deals were struck with other countries too. Japan's isolation and the Edo period came to an end, as the last shogun was toppled from power and the emperor took back control.

The Japanese called the American steamships 'Black Ships' because they pumped out plumes of black smoke.

Russia looks to Europe

Peasant farmers

Like China, Russia had been left in disarray after Mongol invasions during the Middle Ages. It was a vast territory, spanning Asia and Europe, with a wealth of metals, crops and animal pelts to sell. But it was isolated, with few trading routes into Europe. From 1462, a line of rulers, starting with Tsar Ivan III, pushed to modernize Russia and improve links with Europe.

'Tsar', or 'Czar', comes from 'Caesar' – the title given to Roman emperors.

1547-1584
IVAN THE TERRIBLE

Ivan IV earned the nickname, 'Grozny', meaning terrible or fearsome. He had a suspicious, violent nature that led him to kill anyone he distrusted, including his own son and heir.

Ivan built Moscow's famous onion-domed St. Basil's Cathedral to celebrate his victory over descendants of Genghis Khan in Kazan, 800km (500 miles) east of Moscow.

The Tsar recaptured lost territories from the Mongols and seized land from Russia's noble class, the *boyars*.

He also took away all peasants' rights, turning them into serfs who couldn't leave their master's land.

In 1613, after a period of civil war following Ivan's death, the Romanov family took power. This dynasty would rule Russia for 300 years.

Fur trappers

1682-1725
PETER THE GREAT

Peter I, 'the Great', fought Sweden to seize land on the Baltic coast. There, he ordered the construction of a new capital city – St. Petersburg, which he called his 'window on the West' because it was styled as an elegant western European city.

Peter reformed the government and borrowed ideas from Europe to modernize his country.

He brought in engineers, shipbuilders, architects and craftsmen from Europe to help build new canals, factories and ships. He even worked in Dutch and English shipyards to learn from them.

The Tsar forced the boyars to cut off their beards and wear European fashions.

1762-1796
CATHERINE THE GREAT

A renowned, often ruthless leader, Catherine was the German wife of Peter III. Her generals extended Russia's territories south and west. She founded art museums and corresponded with leading European writers.

But while wealthy Russians prospered, life remained hard and hopeless for the millions of peasant serfs, who would not be granted their freedom until 1861.

Main arch of the Taj Mahal, built in Agra, 1632–1653

Muslim empires

During the 1500s, the leaders of three great dynasties dominated the Muslim world. Under the rule of Sultan Suleiman I, 'the Magnificent', from 1520 to 1566, the Ottoman Empire extended south to the borders of Persia, and north into eastern Europe, even threatening Vienna.

Meanwhile, the Mughal dynasty, claiming descent from Genghis Khan, governed most of India. The Mughal *Shah* (ruler), Akbar I, 'the Great', took power in 1556. He inspired loyalty among Hindus as well as Muslims in India by marrying a Hindu princess.

Meanwhile, the Safavid dynasty ruled in Persia. Their powerful Shah Abbas I, 'the Great', drove the Ottomans from his lands in the early 1600s.

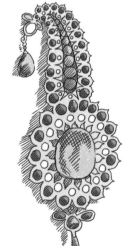

Eastern opulence

These three great empires all amassed staggering wealth, and produced dazzling art and architecture. Their cities, filled with beautiful gardens, palaces, bathhouses and mosques, were cleaner and more advanced than most in Europe at the time.

Skilled craftworkers in the Muslim empires used diamonds, emeralds, rubies and gold to make fine ornaments, such as this brooch for a turban.

GUNPOWDER EMPIRES

Muslim armies were able to conquer large empires because they understood the power of the latest battlefield guns. Their soldiers were armed with muskets and used carts or animals to carry larger, mounted guns into battle.

Ottoman artillery soldier with a cannon

Mughal musketeer

Safavid gunman with a camel-mounted gun

Vienna

Rome

SAFAVID EMPIRE

MUGHAL EMPIRE

Istanbul

Mediterranean Sea

Damascus

Isfahan

Delhi

Jerusalem

Agra

OTTOMAN EMPIRE

Mecca

Arabian Sea

MUSLIM EMPIRES IN THE 1500S

Born to rule

Many European rulers in the 17th and 18th centuries were 'absolute monarchs', meaning their word was law, their every wish was obeyed and their every whim indulged. They had ministers to help them govern, but some rulers chose to ignore them – at great cost.

In 1642, clashes between King Charles I of England and his parliament sparked a terrible civil war, which ended with Charles being beheaded in 1649. The monarchy wasn't restored until 1660, when Charles's son was crowned Charles II.

Royal one-upmanship

Monarchs across Europe were building vast new palaces, lavishly decorated inside and surrounded by elegant gardens and water features. Royal courts competed to have the most flamboyant fashions and entertainments, but by far the most opulent was the French King Louis XIV's palace at Versailles.

Ta-da!

King Louis, your costume is *magnifique!*

Ooh look, the King has dressed up as Apollo, the Greek god of the Sun.

Louis XIV was famous for putting on extravagant dances and operas.

Gunning for each other

More serious competitions took place on the battlefield. In 1700, King Charles II of Spain died. He had no children, so he left his lands to his relative, Philip, the grandson of Louis XIV of France. The English and the Dutch were alarmed that Spain and France might unite and become too powerful, so they formed a 'Grand Alliance' to fight the French.

After 13 years of fighting involving many other European countries, it was finally agreed that Philip could become King of Spain after all, as long as France and Spain remained separate. The Habsburgs still ruled in Austria, but it was the end of their rule in Spain.

An age of ideas

In the 1700s, during times of peace, rich nobles toured around Europe, buying works of art and seeing how others lived.

At home, educated nobles and members of a new 'middle class' of wealthy merchants, business owners and professionals, made studies of plants, animals and natural curiosities, as well as conducting experiments. They held gatherings, or 'salons', in their homes to discuss books and questions about human nature, the best ways to govern and trade, and the rights of all people. This new spirit of curiosity has been called the Enlightenment.

GOING GLOBAL

The newfound sea routes around the world made European merchants fantastically rich. They also opened the way for the first ever multinational companies, and brought people from all corners of the world into contact. For the first time, events on one side of the world could have global repercussions.

A golden age for the Dutch

The Netherlands built up a huge fleet of navy and cargo ships, and became a trading hub for the world. Attracted by its wealth, artists, scientists and craftsmen flocked to the thriving city of Amsterdam.

Dutch ships carried goods from Asia, West Africa and the Americas, and their crews were the only Europeans permitted to trade with Japan. In 1600, the British East India Company was established, to do business around the world. Not to be outdone, the Dutch set up their own company two years later. It had trading bases across Asia and its own private army.

Porcelain ornaments, like this elephant, were made in China and Japan especially to sell to the Dutch.

Striking it rich

Merchants in Amsterdam bought shares, or stocks, in the Dutch East India Company, hoping to sell them later at great profit. This was the beginning of the world's first stock market, as people invested their savings in business ventures.

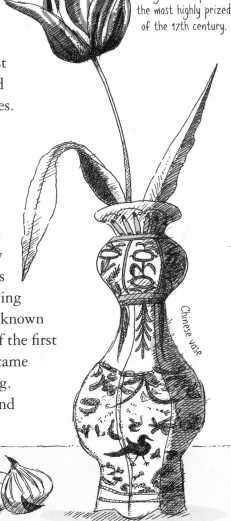

The red and white streaked *Semper Augustus* tulip was the most highly prized of the 17th century.

Tulip mania

When investors all pursued the same stocks, buying grew frenzied. Many Europeans were fascinated by tulips, newly imported from Turkey. Investors traded shares in rare bulbs, driving up their price in a buying fever known as 'tulip mania'. This was one of the first stock bubbles. When prices became too high, people stopped buying. Then prices suddenly crashed and investors lost everything.

Chinese vase

In 1637, a single *Semper Augustus* tulip bulb was sold for as much as a large Amsterdam mansion house.

Tulip bulbs

West African kingdoms

I n West Africa, several advanced kingdoms had grown up in the Middle Ages. They had wealthy cities, efficient governments, their own courts and currencies, and trade routes into the continent.

The Kingdom of Benin (1 on the map opposite) was ruled by a king, or *Oba*. He lived in a palace decorated with bronze plaques depicting religious ceremonies and military victories. His disciplined army was often fighting to conquer more lands, and to bring back prisoners as slaves.

A Benin bronze portrait of a queen

Coastal traders

S tarting in the 1440s, trade links grew between West Africans and Portuguese sailors, who navigated the coast and went on to set up fortified trading posts there. The Portuguese supplied the Oba with brass and copper, in exchange for military protection, ivory, gold and slaves.

Like Benin, the Oyo Kingdom (2) and Ashanti Empire (3) had powerful armies that fought to secure coastal ports and to seize prisoner slaves from local rivals. They grew rich in the 17th and 18th centuries, trading with Dutch slavers for weapons, which they used to wage wars and capture more slaves.

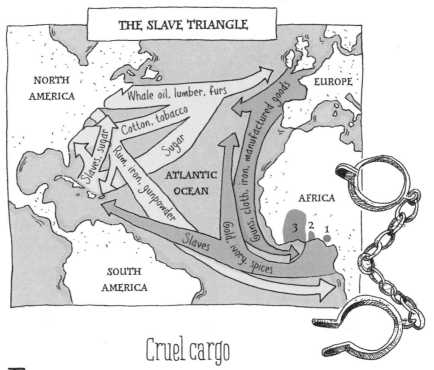

THE SLAVE TRIANGLE

NORTH AMERICA

EUROPE

Whale oil, lumber, furs

Cotton, tobacco

Sugar

Slaves, sugar

Rum, iron, gunpowder

ATLANTIC OCEAN

AFRICA

3 2 1

Gold, ivory, spices

Guns, cloth, iron, manufactured goods

Slaves

SOUTH AMERICA

Cruel cargo

European traders turned slavery into an international industry, shipping ten million or more people across the world. They sailed in a grim triangle, arriving in West Africa with guns and other goods to trade for slaves, before leaving for colonies in the Americas.

The passage was a deadly torment for the human cargo, kept chained in dark, cramped confinement below deck. Many died during the crossing. On arrival, men, women and children were sold to work on plantations. Slave ships departed full of sugar or rum and docked in their home ports before setting out again for Africa.

The transatlantic slave trade was abolished in the 1800s, but remains an unhealed wound in world history.

DATE CHART: THE EARLY MODERN WORLD

	THE AMERICAS	EUROPE
1450	1492: Christopher Columbus reached the West Indies. 1497: John Cabot reached Newfoundland. 1499: Amerigo Vespucci landed in South America.	1450s-1500s: The Renaissance was at its height. 1440s: Johannes Gutenberg developed Europe's first printing press.
1500	1500s: Portuguese settlers arrived in Brazil. 1519-21: Conquistadors conquered the Aztecs.	1517: Martin Luther wrote his 95 Theses, sparking the Reformation. 1522: Magellan and Elcano's voyage was the first to sail all around the globe.
1550	1532-1572: Conquistadors conquered the Incas.	1543: Copernicus published his theory that the planets go around the Sun. 1547-1584: Reign of Ivan the Terrible in Russia
1600	1580s: The transatlantic slave trade began. 1603: French colonists arrived in Canada.	1556: Charles V divided up the Habsburg Empire. 1558-1603: Reign of Elizabeth I in England 1581: The Republic of the United Netherlands was formed.
1650	1620: The Mayflower arrived in North America, bringing settlers from Britain.	1618-1648: The Thirty Years' War 1633: Galileo was sentenced to imprisonment for going against the teaching of the Catholic Church. 1636-1637: Tulip mania
1700	1699: The French set up the colony of Louisiana.	1642-1646: The English Civil War 1643-1715: Reign of Louis XIV in France 1682-1725: Reign of Peter the Great in Russia 1685-1815: The Enlightenment 1701-1714: The War of Spanish Succession
1750	1759: The British captured Quebec from the French.	1762-1796: Reign of Catherine the Great in Russia

AFRICA	ASIA AND AUSTRALASIA
1440s: The Portuguese started trading in West Africa.	
1487: Bartholomeu Dias was the first European to sail around the southern tip of Africa.	**1498:** Vasco da Gama was the first European to sail to India. 
1505: Portuguese traders set up ports on the coast of East Africa.	**1520-1566:** Suleiman I ruled the Ottomans.
1516-1560: Ottoman Turks ruled large areas of North Africa. 	**1556-1605:** Shah Akbar I ruled the Mughal Empire in India.
	1588-1629: Shah Abbas I ruled in Safavid Persia.
	1595: Dutch traders set up ports in the East Indies.
	1600: The British East India Company was created.
	1603-1868: Edo period in Japan
1616: Dutch and French traders set up ports on the coast of West Africa.	**1606:** Dutch explorers reached Australia.
	1642: Dutch explorer Abel Tasman reached New Zealand.
1652: Dutch settlers conquered Cape Colony.	**1644:** The Ming dynasty ended and the Manchu Qing dynasty took over in China.
1700-1800: African Kingdoms of Benin, Oyo and Ashanti were wealthy and powerful. 	**1730:** The Safavid Empire in Persia ended. 

PART FOUR

THE MODERN WORLD

From the 1750s

Speeding into modernity

The pace of change accelerated rapidly from the 1750s, as revolutions in the way people worked and how they were governed brought the world hurtling into the modern age.

Empires and industry

The overseas colonies and empires that European countries had begun to build in the 17th century were a great source of wealth, as well as providing new foods and raw materials. More money and greater resources helped to pay for new inventions and machines that radically changed farming and industry in the 18th and 19th centuries. Soon, fields gave way to factories, cities and electricity plants.

It was the beginning of an industrial age, and an age of great movement, as people were able to travel further, faster than ever before – thanks to the invention of railways, steamships and motor cars.

The age of machines

From the 1750s in Britain, new agricultural machines were invented and new, efficient farming methods were introduced that yielded bigger harvests and a better diet for many. Cities grew, as more and more new inventions and machines transformed the way people lived and worked.

These changes became known as the Industrial Revolution, which took hold first in Britain, providing a model for progress that quickly spread around the globe and shaped the modern age.

In the 1750s, only one in every ten people in Britain lived in cities or towns. The government began turning over common land to large-scale farms. Improved crops, planting methods and machinery made fields more bountiful.

But as farms became more efficient, many farm workers lost their jobs and fled to the cities looking for work.

From the 1780s, coal-fired steam engines were invented to pump water and drive machines.

Britain's mines supplied vast quantities of coal and iron ore to make steel to build the engines.

Work previously done by hand could now be done quickly and precisely by machines in factories. Workers were summoned each morning by steam whistles.

Factory workers, including young children, had to tend the whirring machines. It was dangerous and badly paid, and there were no safety laws to protect them.

Large towns and cities grew up around the factories. Factory workers – members of a new 'working class' – lived in small houses in filthy, overcrowded parts of the city.

To transport goods to and from ports and cities, engineers dug networks of canals and railway lines.

Powerful steam engines were fitted inside trains and ships, bringing an end to the age of sail. Travel overseas became easier and cargo could be transported to distant markets faster than ever before.

Struggle for America

By the 1750s, European powers had claimed large territories across North America: the French in Canada, the Great Lakes and down to Louisiana; the Spanish in Mexico and California; the Russians in Alaska. Much of the land they claimed was little more than a howling wilderness, sparsely populated by native inhabitants, dotted with forts and remote outposts for animal trappers, traders and miners. In contrast, the British had set up 13 colonies along the east coast, all teeming with people, farms and companies.

Colonies in revolt

As they prospered, many British colonists began to resent their rulers in London, who kept a stranglehold on trade by imposing strict laws and taxes, without giving the colonists a say in how they were governed.

In 1773, a band of protestors in the port of Boston stormed a British East India Company ship and hurled its cargo of tea crates overboard. The Boston Tea Party, as it became known, was the beginning of a wave of protests against British rule in America. The British government responded by bringing in even harsher laws, and then by sending troops across the Atlantic. In 1775, the first shots rang out in what developed into the American War of Independence.

Independence Day

As battles raged along the coast, representatives from the 13 colonies gathered in Philadelphia. On July 4, 1776, they agreed on a Declaration of Independence, proclaiming their rights as self-governing states that would bind together as the United States of America.

> We hold these truths to be self-evident, that **all men are created equal**, that they are endowed by their Creator with certain unalienable Rights, that among these are **Life, Liberty** and the pursuit of **Happiness**.

Extract from the Declaration of Independence

Signing the Declaration

In 1781, the British were finally defeated, and in 1789, the USA elected George Washington as its first president. It was the first time a New World colony had thrown off its Old World master, and was the birth of a nation that would become a global superpower.

Britons abroad

Shaken by the loss of their territories in America, the British turned their attention to establishing new colonies and building up existing ones, particularly in Australia, New Zealand, India and Africa.

Convict country

In 1770, Captain James Cook explored the east coast of Australia, claiming it for Britain. The British government hoped that a new colony there would provide a foothold between the Indian Ocean and the Pacific, from where Britain's trading empire could grow.

It would also serve another purpose. Prisons in Britain were ramshackle and overcrowded, so the solution was to send convicts to penal colonies overseas instead. Between 1788 and 1868, at least 160,000 men, women and children would be transported to the far side of the world.

Poachers and murderers were transported for life, but even stealing a pig or a few pennies earned you seven years. On release, convicts had to pay their own passage home – for most, who had little or no money, this meant transportation was a one-way ticket.

Close encounters

The so-called 'First Fleet' of British convict ships landed at Botany Bay, close to present-day Sydney in 1788. Soon, other settlers arrived. Most took land where they could farm sheep and cattle, but others went in search of gold. As the colony prospered and grew, settlers seized ancestral lands that had been home to the Australian Aboriginals for thousands of years. Some tribes were forced to adopt a European way of life. Many were wiped out by smallpox and other diseases that arrived with the settlers.

New Zealand joins the British Empire

Captain Cook had also mapped the islands of New Zealand. From the late 1770s, Britons began settling there, taking land from the local people, the Maoris. In 1840, hundreds of Maori chiefs signed the Treaty of Waitangi, a contract that protected Maori lands and other freedoms, while bringing the country under the rule of Queen Victoria's British Empire. This didn't prevent conflict later, as Maoris struggled to take back land that settlers had seized.

However, within less than a century, as subjects of the Empire, people from New Zealand and Australia would go on to support Britain in two world wars.

REVOLUTIONARY TIMES

In the 1700s, European Enlightenment thinkers urged people to question old ideas, such as the right of kings to live as they pleased. Instead, they demanded fairer laws and more control over their own lives. In France, crowds stormed palaces and took power in a revolution that shook the world.

The people rise up in France

France was on its knees after a run of bad harvests and costly wars. While many starved, King Louis XVI and his nobles lived in pampered luxury, funded by the high taxes peasants and workers were forced to pay. In 1789, riots broke out in Paris and soon the country was in turmoil. In 1793, the rebels executed the King and declared France a republic, governed by and for the people. Hundreds more were executed in a period of violence known as 'the Reign of Terror'.

The rebels used a fearful invention called the guillotine to chop off the heads of their enemies – including the King and Queen.

LIBERTY, EQUALITY AND BROTHERHOOD – OR DEATH.

Emperor Napoleon

Horrified, Europe's rulers sent invading armies to stop the revolution spreading beyond France. But the French had a secret weapon – a brilliant, young military commander, named Napoleon Bonaparte. He led his troops to victories in all corners of Western Europe, and soon he was leading the country too...

1799
Napoleon took control in France. He restored order to France and its colonies by implementing a new code of laws and rights.

1804
Napoleon was crowned Emperor of France.

1805
Britain's powerful navy defeated French ships at the Battle of Trafalgar, preventing Napoleon from invading Britain.

BY 1812
Napoleon had conquered most of western Europe.

1815
Napoleon was finally defeated when British and Prussian troops joined forces to crush his exhausted army at the Battle of Waterloo.

1814
He was captured and imprisoned on the Mediterranean island of Elba, but he escaped and returned to power.

1812
Napoleon invaded Russia, winning several battles, but was forced to retreat at Moscow. Thousands of his men perished on the long march home through the freezing winter snow.

1815-1821
Napoleon was exiled to St. Helena, a wave-lashed island in the South Atlantic, where he eventually died. But his triumphs – and the aftershocks of the French Revolution – continued to be felt across Europe and the wider world.

A year of revolutions

The French Revolution, with its motto of 'liberty, equality and brotherhood', inspired people across Europe to demand more say in the way they were governed. By 1848, the call for change was growing. In many places there weren't enough jobs, and after a run of bad harvests, many faced food shortages too.

In February 1848, a rebellion broke out in Paris, setting off a wave of revolutions in other cities including Vienna, Budapest, Prague, Frankfurt and Naples. These revolutions were crushed, but social and political changes were to prove inevitable.

A sense of identity

While people protested for liberty and equality, some European writers and artists explored ideas of brotherhood, in the form of romantic nationalism – the sense that people from the same region have a national identity based on a shared language and culture. As part of this movement, people such as the brothers Grimm in Germany revived traditional customs and folk tales.

Romantic writers and artists often took inspiration from the natural landscapes of their homelands.

National pride

The gathering pace of nationalism in the 19th century caused the map of Europe to be redrawn. While some nations broke away from previous rulers, other states came together to form new countries.

The Greeks had been ruled by the Ottoman Empire since the 15th century. But in 1821, they began a war of independence. The Ottomans finally recognized Greece as an independent kingdom in 1832.

In Brussels, in 1831, the staging of a nationalistic opera stirred people to riot in the streets against the rule of King William I of the Netherlands. A year later, Belgium was established as an independent kingdom.

Coming together

Germany and Italy were made up of several states. In Italy, where states were ruled by foreign countries, Camillo Benso, Count of Cavour, fought for control in the north, while a soldier named Giuseppe Garibaldi led an army in the south. They agreed to join forces and in 1861 the unified nation of Italy was set up.

The most powerful German state was Prussia, governed by Wilhelm I and his prime minister Otto von Bismarck. They built up the Prussian army and took control of other German states. In 1871, the remaining states decided to join them, and Germany was born, with Wilhelm as its first emperor, or *kaiser*.

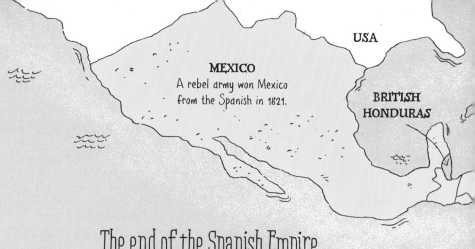

MEXICO
A rebel army won Mexico
from the Spanish in 1821.

USA

BRITISH
HONDURAS

The end of the Spanish Empire

Not many people have been able to say they have a country named after them, but Bolivia took its name from Símon Bolívar, a dashing cavalry general who freed the region from Spanish rule.

Bolívar started his revolutionary charge across South America in the early 1800s. After driving the colonial occupiers from his homeland of Venezuela, he went on to liberate Panama, Colombia, Ecuador and northern Peru, battling a Spanish military that was weakened and distracted by Napoleon's rampages in Europe.

Crossing the continent

While Bolívar's troops advanced from the north, an Argentine freedom fighter, José de San Martín, led an army across the Andes Mountains to help free Chile and join a triumphant Bolívar in Peru. It was the first taste of independence for millions of South Americans along the whole length of the continent, after 400 years of taking orders from Spain.

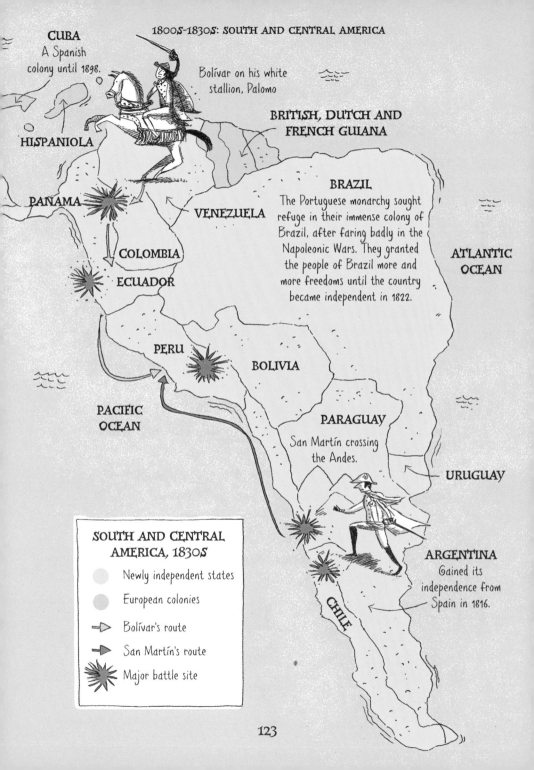

CUBA
A Spanish
colony until 1898.

Bolívar on his white
stallion, Palomo

HISPANIOLA

**BRITISH, DUTCH AND
FRENCH GUIANA**

PANAMA

VENEZUELA

BRAZIL
The Portuguese monarchy sought
refuge in their immense colony of
Brazil, after faring badly in the
Napoleonic Wars. They granted
the people of Brazil more and
more freedoms until the country
became independent in 1822.

COLOMBIA

ECUADOR

**ATLANTIC
OCEAN**

PERU

BOLIVIA

**PACIFIC
OCEAN**

PARAGUAY

San Martín crossing
the Andes.

URUGUAY

**SOUTH AND CENTRAL
AMERICA, 1830S**

- Newly independent states
- European colonies
- ⇨ Bolívar's route
- ➡ San Martín's route
- ✴ Major battle site

ARGENTINA
Gained its
independence from
Spain in 1816.

CHILE

Settlers in America

The newly independent United States was a country rich in raw materials and farmland, with a culture of hard work and invention. The nation prospered and grew, tempting millions of Europeans to its shores in search of a better life.

Migrants came for the jobs in thriving cities and to settle in the frontier territories known as the West, establishing new states. Most saw this as a vast empire of land ripe for the taking. When gold was discovered in California in 1848, wagonloads of people rushed to the area, hoping to make their fortunes.

Settlers and Native Americans

Settlers and US soldiers forced over a million Native Americans from their homelands. Some tribes fought hard to keep their land, winning a few battles, but they lacked the numbers and the firepower to resist the US army. Some tribes were wiped out entirely, and by the 1890s many had been marched to live in large, often barren, reservations guarded by US soldiers.

A wagon train arrives in Native American land in the West.

Union
soldier

Confederate
soldier

The Civil War

In 1860, Abraham Lincoln was elected US President. By that time, there were 33 American states. Many northern states had cities and factories, while most southern states made their money from cotton and tobacco, grown on plantations that relied on slave workers. Lincoln wanted to abolish slavery. In response, the southern states decided to set up their own government, the Confederacy. What followed was the bloodiest war in American history.

There was terrible slaughter on both sides, with half a million killed. The Confederates had fine generals, but the Union troops of the North had more men, better weapons and a joined-up rail network. After four years, the rebel states surrendered. They rejoined the United States and slavery was abolished.

Land of the free

Just five days after the war ended, a supporter of slavery assassinated President Lincoln. It was a foretaste of the struggles ahead, as black people continued to be unjustly treated, especially in the South. However, by the late 19th century, the United States was growing rich and powerful, with electric light and energy coming to its cities, and train lines opening up the West.

From the 1880s, many immigrants' first glimpse of the US as they sailed into New York was that towering symbol of freedom, the Statue of Liberty.

A last rush for empire

Britain's East India Company had been trading in India since the 1600s. It gained control of ports and set up colonies, gradually taking over more and more land. The Company recruited local soldiers, or *sepoys*, to keep order – but in 1857 the men mutinied.

Opening shots

The sepoys belonged to India's main religious groups, Hindus and Muslims. Many felt the British didn't respect their religions, and grew resentful of the land taxes and changes they had introduced. So, when soldiers in Bengal turned fire on their commanders, fighting quickly spread, as thousands of rebels seized towns and torched British-owned farms.

After loyal troops broke up the rebellion, the British government took over direct rule from the company. This was known as the *Raj*, an Indian word for 'rule', with a viceroy appointed by Queen Victoria to oversee India's provinces and princely states. Many Indians campaigned for independence, but the Raj remained in power for almost a century.

The Scramble for Africa

In the 1800s, Africa became a distant chess board, where conflicts brewing inside Europe were played out. European powers made a frenzied rush to snatch land for their empires, also hoping to find gold and riches. This became known as the 'Scramble for Africa'.

Local people, such as the Zulus in the south, fought back, but soon vast areas were in European hands. In 1884, Europe's leaders met in Berlin and decided to carve up the continent of almost ten million square miles between them. Many Africans rebelled, suffering hardships and harsh treatment by their new rulers.

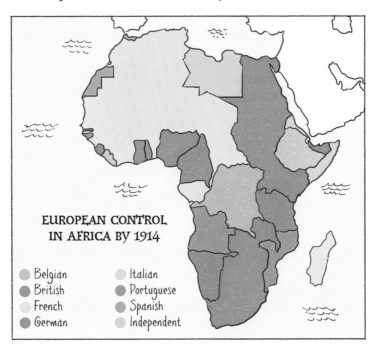

EUROPEAN CONTROL
IN AFRICA BY 1914

- Belgian
- British
- French
- German
- Italian
- Portuguese
- Spanish
- Independent

A brighter future

Life was often dirty and difficult in the industrial towns that grew up during the 19th century. But by the turn of the 20th century, a wave of inventions and innovations had started to bring greater freedoms, improved health and new forms of entertainment.

World fairs, or expositions, drew visitors in their thousands, as manufacturers and scientists proudly displayed the very latest inventions.

HEALTH AND SANITATION

1840S: Anaesthetics were first used in surgery.
1858: The 'Great Stink' (caused by large amounts of waste piling up in London) led engineers and town planners to develop modern sewer systems.
1864: The Red Cross Society was founded in Geneva, to provide care for war casualties.
1865: French chemist Louis Pasteur published his theory that germs cause diseases.
1860S–70S: In Britain, Joseph Lister brought in the use of antiseptics and sterilization in hospitals.
1895: German physicist Wilhelm Röntgen discovered X-rays.
1896: Radiation therapy was introduced for cancer patients.

By the late 1800s, medics were wearing white gowns and masks, washing their hands and using antiseptic spray to help prevent the spread of diseases in hospitals.

Look! No germs.

TRANSPORTATION

1837: The first transatlantic steamship was launched.
1863: The first underground railway opened in London.
1880s: The first 'safety' bicycles with brakes and
gears were manufactured in England and the US.
1885: The world's first motor car was built.
1903: American brothers Orville and Wilbur Wright
made the first powered flight.
1903: Henry Ford introduced the first mass-production
techniques in his new car factory.

German husband and
wife Karl and Bertha
Benz built the world's
first motor car.

LIGHT, SOUND AND VISION

1837: Louis Daguerre invented daguerrotype photographs.
1876: Alexander Graham Bell made the first telephone call.
1877: Thomas Edison produced the first musical phonograph.
1879: The light bulb was patented by Thomas Edison.
1881: Emile Berliner patented a gramophone.
1888: George Eastman produced the Kodak No. 1 camera.
1895: The Lumière brothers showed ten short movies in Paris.
1900s: Guglielmo Marconi set up the first radio factory.

Hold still...
and smile!

Several scientists invented light bulbs
around the same time as Edison, but
he was the first to patent his design.

Crisis for China

After a period of growth under Manchu emperors of the Qing dynasty, China ran into a storm of catastrophes in the 19th century. Its population had surged to 400 million, but harvests were too small to feed the hungry. Famine and rebellion spread across the land, while foreign powers – French, British, Russian and Japanese – pressed at the borders, threatening war.

China had once been the envy of the world for its advanced civilization and scientific progress, but now the Empire had fallen behind the industrial nations. Its armies and ships were too weak to stop the British from taking important trading ports, such as Hong Kong, and gaining control of China's trade.

End of empire

Millions of people starved or died in revolts against the emperor, leaving warlords free to seize vast regions. By the turn of the century, most people in China accepted that their country must adapt and change its ways if it wanted to survive in the modern age.

In 1911-1912, there was a revolution in China. The last emperor was forced from his throne in the Forbidden City, ending two thousand years of tradition and rule.

Emperor Puyi was just six years old when he was deposed.

Japan moves with the times

In Japan, Emperor Meiji took power in 1868, after two centuries of rule by the shoguns. He replaced his samurai fighters with a modern army and built a navy to rival the American warships that had led Japan to reopen its borders. Borrowing methods of teaching, business and law, Japan transformed into a great, industrial power at breakneck speed.

The Japanese looked to foreign lands and the spoils of war. Following quick victories in China, Japan's military commanders shocked the world by smashing Russian forces in 1904 and marching into Manchuria.

KEY EVENTS IN CHINA AND JAPAN

1839-1842: The Opium War – a trade dispute between China and Britain.

1850-1864: The Taiping Rebellion attempted to overthrow the Qing in China, in fighting that led to the deaths of up to 20 million people.

1854: The Japanese signed a trade deal with the US.

1868: In Japan, the emperor took back control from the shogun.

1880s: Japanese engineers started building steam trains.

1894-1895: Japan fought China for control of Korea.

1900: Rebels attacked foreigners in China in the Boxer Rebellion.

1904-1905: Japan fought Russia over rival claims for Manchuria and Korea.

1912: The Qing were overthrown and China became a republic.

THE WORLD AT WAR

Tension that had been building in Europe since the 1880s finally exploded into all-out war in 1914. A Bosnian Serb group wanting independence from Austria-Hungary murdered the heir to the Austrian Empire, sparking threats of war between nations bound together by military pacts. France, Russia and Britain gathered their forces against Germany, Austria-Hungary and the fading Ottoman Empire. Both sides refused to back down, believing their armies to be invincible. Nobody imagined the horrors to come.

All over by Christmas

When a German army invaded Belgium and France, soldiers dug trenches to protect themselves from bullets and bombs. Within weeks, a jagged line of opposing trenches snaked from the English Channel to the borders of Switzerland.

Confident commanders predicted a swift victory, claiming the war would be over by Christmas. But fighting continued in these muddy trenches for much of the next four years, claiming millions of lives.

THE TECHNOLOGY OF WAR

A vast array of new technology was developed and mobilized as part of the war effort. Here are some of the inventions used for the first time on a wide scale in the First World War:

Tanks
Flame-throwers
Two-way pilot radios
Mobile X-ray units
Aircraft carriers

Poison gas
Pilotless reconnaissance drones
Depth charges for submarines
Steel helmets
Stainless steel

Nowhere to hide

What began as a European war rapidly became a global conflict. Naval battles took place on distant seas, while submarines and bomber aircraft attacked ships and cities. Soldiers were recruited from European colonies, and fighting spread to parts of Africa, the Middle East and the Far East, where the Europeans had interests to protect. Known at the time as the Great War, it is now called the First World War.

A bitter peace

The United States joined the conflict in 1917, supporting Britain and France. Outnumbered and with food shortages causing riots at home, Germany and its allies surrendered in 1918. The German people struggled to pay fines imposed by the victors, leaving wounds and grievances that would have a terrible legacy.

The Red Star rises

Meanwhile, Russia had crashed out of the conflict in 1917, and was facing a civil war, after a startling revolution that had toppled its ruler, Tsar Nicholas II.

In November 1917, a revolutionary group, led by an activist known as Lenin, seized power. Lenin followed the ideas of Karl Marx, a 19th-century German thinker who wrote that workers should overthrow their masters and build a Communist or Socialist state, with every person sharing the nation's land, industry and wealth.

The Soviet Union

Lenin gave land to the peasants and put workers in charge of the factories. Many Russians were opposed to these changes, so this led to a civil war, during which the Tsar and his family, the Romanovs, were assassinated.

In 1922, after the fighting had ended, Russia was renamed the Union of Soviet Socialist Republics (USSR) or the Soviet Union.

Vladimir Ilyich Ulyanov, better known as Lenin, is shown here by the flag of the Soviet Union. The red star is a symbol of the Communist Party. The hammer stands for industry and the sickle stands for agriculture.

Workers of the world, unite!

Farms in the Soviet Union were joined together to create vast farms called collectives.

Stalin's iron rule

Under the rule of Lenin's successor Josef Stalin, the Soviet Union became a strong industrial nation with factories, steelworks and railways. But he was a ruthless, paranoid leader, who executed his enemies, and caused the deaths of as many as 40 million Soviet people.

China's Long March

In China, civil war broke out in 1927 between the Kuomintang, or Nationalist Party, and the Communist Party. In 1934, the Kuomintang army surrounded and attacked the Communist-held Jiangxi province in southeast China. The Communists decided to escape, and head north to find a safe place. Their arduous trek, the Long March, of over 8,000km (5,000 miles) was made on foot, and of the 100,000 people who set out, 70,000 died. The Communists' determination and their strong leader Mao Zedong inspired many young people to join them, but it wasn't until 1949 that the Communists eventually gained control in China.

The Jazz Age

With the war over, governments worked to rebuild their countries and bring back the living standards that many had started to achieve in the early years of the century. In the rich trading nations, mass production in factories meant more people could afford cars, radios and telephones. The US in particular enjoyed boom times, with new music, fashions and growing independence for women, in an era called the Jazz Age. It was a giddy flash of light and hope after the terrors of war, but it was gone all too soon.

From boom to bust

In 1929, the value of banks and companies across America collapsed under the weight of hidden debts and weak global trade. This disaster was named after New York's financial district – the Wall Street Crash. But its effects were felt around the world, in what became known as the Great Depression. Factories closed and millions lost their jobs. Many were forced from their homes, and had to wait in line for a meal from charity soup kitchens.

Hitler spread his policies, giving impassioned speeches at mass rallies throughout Germany.

Politics of hate

As the crisis spread, extreme nationalists, or 'fascists', began to stir up hate, blaming minority groups for the world's problems. Fascist leaders, including Benito Mussolini in Italy and Adolf Hitler in Germany, claimed that a tough approach to law and order would create jobs and wealth. They strengthened their military forces and set themselves up as dictators.

Spain became a republic in 1931, but the people were divided and civil war broke out. Rebels led by General Franco, who was supported by Hitler and Mussolini, dropped explosives on civilians from new bomber aircraft. Franco ruled over Spain as a dictator for more than 30 years.

Lighting the fire

Hitler's Nazi Party turned Germany into a war machine, producing weapons and troops. In September 1939, they invaded Poland and then dragged the world into another terrible conflict – the Second World War...

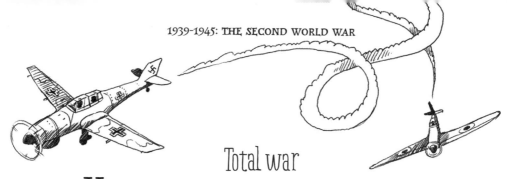

Total war

Hitler raced his troops across Europe, burning and plundering cities, murdering anyone that stood in their way. The Nazis hounded Jews and minority groups, stealing their possessions and sending them to prison camps. Hitler made pacts with other nations, including Italy and Japan, who together formed a group called the Axis Powers.

Island fortress

By 1940, Britain was one of the last free countries in Western Europe, fighting as part of the Allies – the group opposed to the Axis. German submarines hunted British ships, while swarms of Germany's *Luftwaffe* aircraft bombed factories, military bases and homes.

Britain fought on and called for aid. Many men from the old colonies answered the call – from Canada, India, Australia and many other countries.

Clash of the dictators

In 1941, four million German soldiers marched into the Soviet Union. Most never returned, perishing in the bitter cold and colossal battles with Soviet troops.

Waking the giant

At the same time, in Southeast Asia the Japanese had the upper hand over the Allies. But on December 7, 1941, they made the fatal mistake of attacking the US naval base at Pearl Harbor. The Americans thundered into the war, sending armies to the Pacific and Europe.

In June 1944, the Allies landed in France, boosted by fresh troops from the US. Trapped between the advancing Soviet Union and the Allies, Hitler killed himself and Germany surrendered in May 1945.

The desperate end

Meanwhile, Japan's leaders resolved to fight to the last man. But in August 1945, they were forced to surrender after the US unleashed a terrible new weapon – an atomic bomb – on Hiroshima and Nagasaki. The cities were blown to dust in a blinding flash, with a final death toll of 185,000. The Second World War ended under the cloud of a new, and terrifying, nuclear age.

THE HOLOCAUST
It was a war full of outrages, but the Nazis' most evil crimes were against the Jewish people. Six million Jews, and millions of other people, were murdered in the war years, many in Nazi concentration camps. Some of these camps have been preserved and you can visit them today. They stand in permanent memory to the dead, and to remind us all to resist hatred and intolerance.

An uneasy peace

After the war, an organization called the United Nations was set up to promote international peace. One of the UN's first acts was to grant a safe and independent homeland to the Jewish people after the atrocities they had experienced at the hands of the Nazis. Palestine, then an Arab state under British control, was divided to create the Jewish state of Israel.

Many Palestinians, supported by nearby Arab nations, resented the loss of their lands. Israel has fought a series of brutal wars for survival, and clashes over its borders rumble on today.

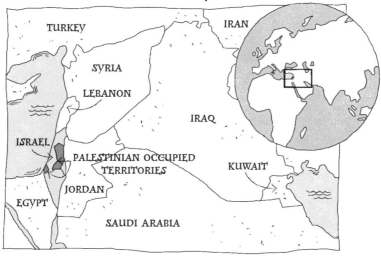

Since the war, the Middle East has seen a number of invasions and territorial disputes, often fuelled by religious differences, as well as conflicts over possession of the region's valuable oil fields.

Taking sides

America and the Soviet Union had been allies during the war, but relations between these two 'superpowers' soon grew frosty. After the war, half of Germany and much of Eastern Europe remained under Soviet control behind an 'Iron Curtain' of minefields, barbed wire and border checkpoints stretching from the Baltic to the Black Sea.

Fearing that the Soviets wanted to take over Europe, the US and Western European powers formed the North Atlantic Treaty Organization, NATO, to defend each other if one of them was attacked. The Cold War, as it became known, was a tense period of threats, stand-offs and mistrust that lasted for next 40 years.

COLD WAR DATES

1949: NATO was formed. Germany was split into two countries. In East Germany, Berlin was split into East and West.
1950-1953: The Korean War
1955-1975: The Vietnam War

1955: The Warsaw Pact formed by the USSR and Eastern European countries.
1961: The Berlin Wall was built.
1962: The Cuban Missile Crisis
1979: The Soviet Union invaded Afghanistan.

WESTERN BLOC
(MEMBERS OF NATO)

EASTERN BLOC
(WARSAW PACT COUNTRIES)

India wakes to freedom

Some two and a half million Indians had fought as part of the British armed forces in the Second World War. In return, the British government promised it would grant independence to India after the war.

At the stroke of midnight on August 15, 1947, India became independent, but it was also divided into two countries. The mainly Hindu part became India; the mainly Muslim parts became East and West Pakistan. However, during this 'Partition', millions of people were forced to move from one state to the other. About 12 million became refugees, and hundreds of thousands died in the chaos and violence that followed.

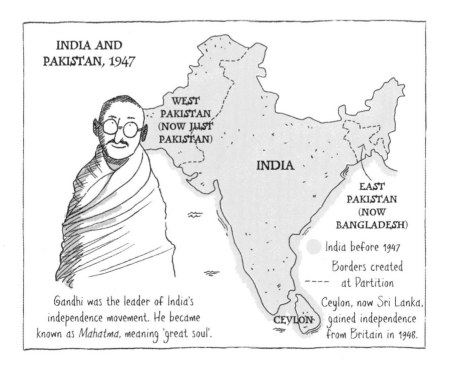

INDIA AND PAKISTAN, 1947

WEST PAKISTAN (NOW JUST PAKISTAN)

INDIA

EAST PAKISTAN (NOW BANGLADESH)

India before 1947

Borders created at Partition

Ceylon, now Sri Lanka, gained independence from Britain in 1948.

CEYLON

Gandhi was the leader of India's independence movement. He became known as *Mahatma*, meaning 'great soul'.

People on the move

In the wake of the war, cities across Europe lay in ruins, and families had lost their homes. Many emigrated to places such as Australia, New Zealand and America to start new lives. Meanwhile, the British government invited people from its colonies and former colonies to help rebuild the country. In 1948, the *Empire Windrush* sailed from Jamaica to Britain, bringing the first wave of hopeful immigrants.

Winds of change

Until the 1950s, much of Africa was still under European colonial rule, but there were increasing calls for change. In 1951, Libya became the first African country to claim independence, and over the next 30 years, more than 40 countries followed suit.

In some places, this happened peacefully, but in others, rebel soldiers fought fiercely against their rulers, and civil wars broke out between rival groups before and after independence was finally achieved.

Civil rights

The post-war years brought a wave of protest and change, as people in many places took to the streets demanding equal rights for all, regardless of race, religion or sex. It was a time of hope and confidence, but still haunted by wars and terrible acts of violence.

Black rights

In the 1950s and 1960s, the United States was still a divided country. In many southern states, black people were forced to sit apart from white people in restaurants, buses and other public places and some state laws acted against them.

Church minister, Martin Luther King Jr. led peaceful marches and demonstrations campaigning for an end to racism. This was part of the nationwide Civil Rights Movement, supported by US President John F. Kennedy. The Civil Rights cause triumphed, but both men paid for their beliefs with their lives – shot dead by crazed assassins.

"I have a dream that one day this nation will rise up and live out the true meaning of its creed: *'We hold these truths to be self-evident, that all men are created equal.'* ... I have a dream that my four little children will one day live in a nation where they will not be judged by the color of their skin but by the content of their character."

An extract from a speech given by Martin Luther King Jr. on August 28, 1963 in which he cited the Declaration of Independence (see page 115).

A year that shook the world

The year 1968 – the year the Martin Luther King Jr. was assassinated – was one of unprecedented civil unrest. Around the world, young people in particular marched for causes including racial equality, women's rights and an end to nuclear weapons. A revolution in attitudes and expectations was underway.

Throughout the United States, and in major cities elsewhere, students staged protests against the war that was being fought in the jungles of Vietnam, where American troops were fighting, and civilians were suffering. In Mexico, Brazil, Spain, Czechoslovakia, and Poland protesters attempted to resist repressive governments. Many of these protests turned violent.

Youth culture

Away from the battlefields and marches, young people were dancing to a new kind of music that promised to break all the rules – rock 'n' roll. Ideas, music and fashion were spreading quicker than ever, by radio, television and vinyl records. Bands played to huge audiences at the first ever rock festivals, and young designers and artists experimented with new styles.

145

Behind the Great Wall

In 1966 Mao Zedong, who had gained control in China soon after the Second World War, launched a campaign called the Cultural Revolution. His aim was to assert his authority and to prevent the people from moving away from communism.

Schools and universities were shut, and young people were encouraged to criticize their bosses and parents. Gangs of teenage fighters, known as Red Guards, beat and tortured anyone they thought was opposed to the regime. It finally ended when Mao died in 1976, but China would take years to recover from the economic chaos and catastrophic loss of life caused by the Cultural Revolution.

New regimes

In 1985, a new leader, Mikhail Gorbachev, came to power in the Soviet Union. He wanted to modernize the country, so he allowed people to set up their own businesses and to vote in free elections for the first time. He also made it clear that the Soviet Union would no longer support other Communist leaders to stay in power in Eastern Europe.

In 1988, thousands of workers in Poland went on strike in protest about their Communist government. Leaders were forced to hold elections. By 1990, Poland had non-communists as prime minister and president.

Walls come down

In 1989 the government in East Germany agreed to lift restrictions on travel to the West. In Berlin, people climbed the wall that split the city into East and West. The gates were opened and thousands flooded through.

The Cold War finally ended in street parties at the start of the 1990s. States broke away from the disintegrating Soviet Union, and the 'Iron Curtain' that had divided Europe since the Second World War came down. Across Eastern Europe, democratic governments were set up, and the old missile bases were left to rust.

Apartheid in Africa

South Africa was blighted by racist laws and attitudes, in a system known as apartheid, which banned black people from voting and segregated them from white people. Nelson Mandela was jailed for 27 years for trying to end racial injustice.

By 1989, under pressure from the United Nations and campaigners around the world, South Africa's government began introducing fairer laws, and a year later Mandela was released. He went on to become the first black president of his country.

Space age

During the Cold War, the USA and the Soviet Union raced to be the first to send a person into space. The Soviets won the race in 1961, but in 1969 the Americans took the next dramatic step...

Around the world, people watched as US astronaut, Neil Armstrong became the first person to walk on the Moon. Since then, there have been numerous missions to space, enabling scientists to find out more about the Universe as well as our own planet.

One small step for Man, one giant leap for mankind.

Crisis and hope

Daily life has changed dramatically in the last 50 years. Breakthroughs in medical science have improved health and quality of life, contributing to a population explosion. Meanwhile, advances in transport, communications, computer and information technology have transformed people's work and leisure.

However, modern life has taken its toll. Fumes and waste pollute our air and seas, natural resources are being used up and the burning of fuel is causing the Earth's temperature to rise, triggering catastrophic storms and droughts. Scientists, pressure groups and politicians are now working hard to protect the planet.

New frontiers

While millions now enjoy a richer and safer way of life than previous generations, many people struggle with poverty, military conflict and hunger – and there is a long way to go before everyone enjoys the rights and freedoms hard-won by those who came before us. But, if we can harness the best of human science, good will and imagination, we can work together towards the brightest future for our world.

Human curiosity, invention and perseverance have carried us from ocean crossings to our first journeys into space. Who knows where we will get to next?

The International Space Station, first launched in 1998, is a research lab that orbits the Earth. Built and staffed by scientists from around the world, it's not only a great scientific achievement, but also a symbol of global cooperation.

DATE CHART: THE MODERN WORLD

DATES	THE AMERICAS	EUROPE
1750	1763: Britain took control in Canada. 1773: The Boston Tea Party 1775-1783: The American War of Independence JULY 4, 1776: The Declaration of Independence 1789: George Washington was elected first President of the USA.	1750s: The Industrial Revolution began first in Britain, then spread around the world. 1789-1799: The French Revolution
1800	1816-1824: Bolívar and San Martín fought for independence for many countries in South America. 1822: Brazil gained independence from Portugal. 1848: The Gold Rush in California	1799-1815: Napoleon Bonaparte ruled France and led his troops in several battles across Europe. 1821-1832: Greek War of Independence from Ottoman rule
1850	1861-1865: The American Civil War 1876: Scotsman Alexander Graham Bell patented the telephone. 1888: Slavery ended throughout the Americas.	1848: Revolutions took place in many parts of Europe. 1861: Italy formed 1871: Germany formed 1885: Karl and Bertha Benz built the world's first motor car in Germany.
1900		1895: X-rays were discovered.

AFRICA	ASIA	AUSTRALASIA

1757-1857: Through the British East India Company, Britain gained control of large parts of India.

1768-1779: Captain James Cook went on three voyages to Australia, New Zealand and the Hawaiian Islands.

1788-1868: British convicts transported to penal colonies in Australia.

1806: Britain took control of Cape Colony in South Africa.

1840: Treaty of Waitangi signed, giving Britain control of New Zealand.

1857-1858: The Indian Mutiny ended with the British taking control in India.

1868: Emperor Meiji took back rule of Japan from the shogun.

1878: Zulus defeated Boers (Dutch settlers) and British fought the Zulus to take their land.

1884-1885: At the Berlin Conference, Europeans agreed to divide Africa between them.

1885: The Indian National Congress was set up to campaign for Indian independence from Britain.

1894-1895: War between China and Japan

1893: Women in New Zealand became the first in the world to be given the right to vote.

DATE CHART: THE MODERN WORLD

DATES	THE AMERICAS	EUROPE
1900	1903: Orville and Wilbur Wright, made the first powered flight.	
		1914-1918: The First World War
	1917: The US joined the First World War.	1917: The Russian Revolution
	1920s: The Jazz Age	
	1929: The Wall Street Crash led to a worldwide Great Depression	
	1941: The US joined the Second World War.	1939-1945: The Second World War
	1945: The UN was founded.	1948: Communists came to power in Czechoslovakia, Hungary, Poland, Romania and Bulgaria.
1950		FROM 1949: Germany was divided into East and West.
	1958: The microchip was invented.	1953: The structure of DNA was discovered by British scientists.
	1962: The Cuban Missile Crisis	1957: The European Economic Community was founded
	1963: US President Kennedy was assassinated.	1961: Yuri Gagarin of the Soviet Union became the first person in space.
	1968: Martin Luther King was assassinated	
	1969: The first Moon landing	
	1981: The US Space Shuttle made its first flight.	1989-1990: Poland elected its first non-communist prime minister and president
		1989: Fall of the Berlin Wall
		1989: Tim Berners-Lee invented the World Wide Web.
	1992: The Earth Summit was held in Rio de Janeiro, Brazil.	1991: The Soviet Union broke up.
		1991-1995: War in Yugoslavia
		1998-1999: War in Kosovo
2000		

DATE CHART: THE MODERN WORLD

AFRICA	ASIA	AUSTRALASIA
1899-1902: The Boer Wars ended with the British defeating the Boers to take control in South Africa.	1904-1905: War was fought between Japan and Russia. 1910: Japan gained control of Korea. 1911-1912: The Chinese Revolution 1918: End of the Ottoman Empire 1920: Gandhi began campaigning for Indian independence. 1922: The Republic of Turkey was formed.	1914-1918: Troops from Australia and New Zealand fought in the First World War.
Gandhi was assassinated by a Hindu extremist in Delhi, in 1948.		
1949: Apartheid was introduced in South Africa. 1951: Libya became independent. 1952-1955: Rebellion in Kenya against British rule 1957: Ghana became independent. 1960s-1980s: Most African states became independent. 1967-1970: The Nigerian Civil War	1947: India and Pakistan became independent. 1948: Israel created 1948-49: Arab-Israeli War 1950-1953: The Korean War 1955-1975: The Vietnam War 1956: Second Arab-Israeli War 1966-1976: China's Cultural Revolution 1967: The Six-Day War between Israel and Arab States 1971: Bangladesh was formed. 1973: The Yom Kippur War between Israel and Arab States	1939-1945: Troops from Australia and New Zealand fought in the Second World War. 
1990-1991: Apartheid ended in South Africa. 1994-1999: Nelson Mandela was President of South Africa.	1980-1988: Iran-Iraq War 1989: Chinese protestors were killed in Tiananmen Square. 1990-1991: Gulf War 1993: Peace agreement between Israel and the Palestinians	1993: Land was returned to Australian Aboriginal people by the Native Title Bill.

Index

Internet Links

For links to websites that bring history alive with virtual tours, video clips and visits to online museums, go to the Usborne Quicklinks website at www.usborne.com/quicklinks and enter the keywords 'short history of the world'. Please follow the internet safety guidelines at the Usborne Quicklinks website.

HERE ARE SOME OF THE THINGS YOU CAN DO AT THE WEBSITES WE RECOMMEND:

* Explore virtual reconstructions of ancient cities and palaces.
* Find out more about the people and events described in this book.
* Watch video clips about major events in world history.
* Examine treasures in museums around the world.

Managing designer: Stephen Moncrieff   Additional design: Jamie Ball & Ian McNee

First published in 2018 by Usborne Publishing Ltd., Usborne House, 83–85 Saffron Hill, London, EC1N 8RT, United Kingdom.